Becky May has led various children's and youth groups and programmes over the past 20 years, including Sunday morning discipleship groups for children aged 0–12 and midweek outreach groups for both primary-age children and teenagers. She was a primary school teacher for eight years, teaching in both Key Stage 1 and 2 and fulfilling leadership responsibilities, before leaving teaching to have her son, Isaac, in September 2012. More recently, the family has grown again following the arrival of baby Keziah. She has written for *Youthwork* magazine, YFC, Urban Saints, UCB and One Way UK, creating a variety of curriculum materials, articles, children's devotional materials and assembly scripts. Becky is also the Bedfordshire Regional Coordinator for Messy Church and cofounder of The Treasurebox People.

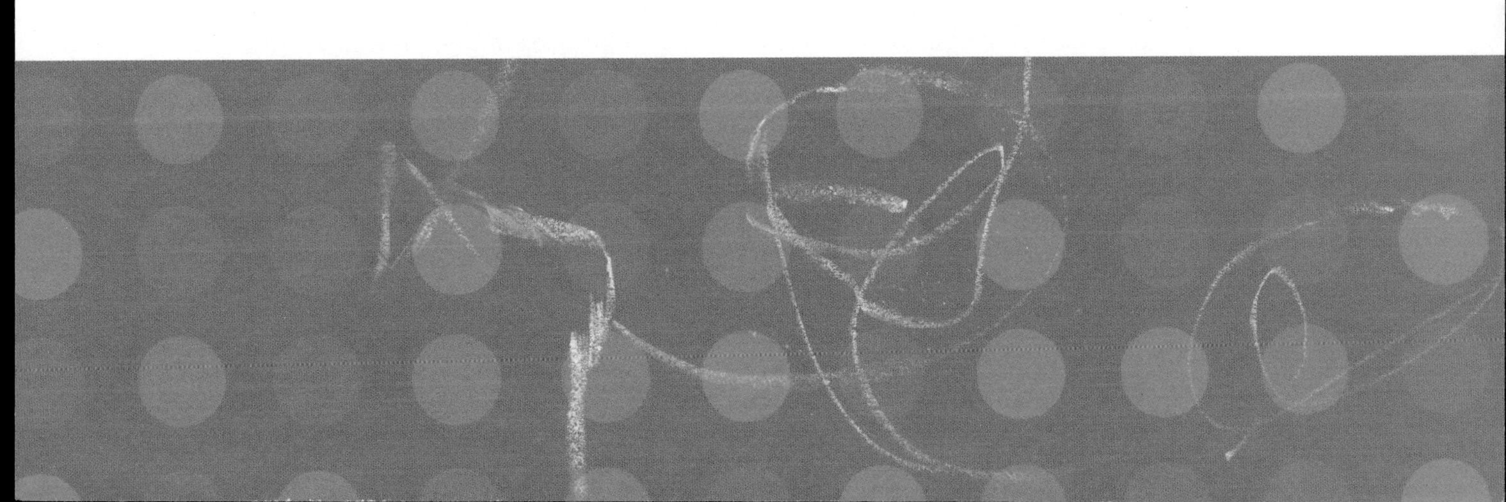

Published by
The Bible Reading Fellowship (BRF)
15 The Chambers, Vineyard
Abingdon OX14 3FE
United Kingdom
Tel: +44 (0)1865 319700
Email: enquiries@brf.org.uk
Website: www.brf.org.uk
BRF is a Registered Charity

ISBN 978 0 85746 425 5

First published 2016
10 9 8 7 6 5 4 3 2 1 0

Acknowledgements
Cover photo: © Thinkstock

Every effort has been made to trace and contact copyright owners for material used in this resource. We apologise for any inadvertent omissions or errors, and would ask those concerned to contact us so that full acknowledgement can be made in the future.

A catalogue record for this book is available from the British Library

Printed by Gutenberg Press, Tarxien, Malta

Important information

Photocopying permission

The right to photocopy material in *God's Story for 5–7s* is granted for the pages that contain the photocopying clause: 'Reproduced with permission from *God's Story for 5–7s* by Becky May (Barnabas for Children, 2016) www.barnabasinchurches.org.uk', so long as reproduction is for use in a teaching situation by the original purchaser. The right to photocopy material is not granted for anyone other than the original purchaser without written permission from BRF.

The Copyright Licensing Agency (CLA)

If you are resident in the UK and you have a photocopying licence with the Copyright Licensing Agency (CLA) please check the terms of your licence. If your photocopying request falls within the terms of your licence, you may proceed without seeking further permission. If your request exceeds the terms of your CLA licence, please contact the CLA directly with your request. Copyright Licensing Agency, Saffron House, 6–10 Kirby Street, London EC1N 8TS UK, Tel: 020 7400 3100, email cla@cla.co.uk; web www.cla.co.uk. The CLA will provide photocopying authorisation and royalty fee information on behalf of BRF.

The Bible Reading Fellowship (BRF) is a Registered Charity (233280).

GOD'S STORY FOR 5–7s

36 Bible-based sessions for midweek and Sunday groups

Contents

Old Testament stories

New Testament stories

Introduction

This book is the second in a series of three, providing a creative curriculum for children to explore God's story through a wide variety of activities, appropriate to different learning styles and preferences. This book provides a curriculum for children aged 5–7 years of age, with a combination of play-based and creative activities that they can use to respond to the story in their own ways.

Who is this book for?

This curriculum has been prepared for those who share God's story with children aged 5–7 years. It could be used as a year-long programme to work through the big story of the Bible week by week, throughout the academic year, or the appropriate stories may be used to celebrate key festivals in the church calendar, with other sessions slotted in as best suits your teaching plan for the year. It is hoped that the book will stimulate your planning to incorporate a wider selection of activities to take account of children's different learning styles.

The materials can be used with a midweek group or as part of a Sunday morning programme, alongside the main Sunday service. For smaller, mixed age groups, you may prefer to combine some elements from this book with those contained in the other two books in the series.

The 36 sessions, which run in sequence, work together to tell God's big story from creation to Pentecost, meeting many of the key stories of the faith along the way. Although there is not space to include every Bible story, the selection builds together to form the overall narrative of God's story.

Activity areas

Each session provides a selection of different activities for the children to engage with, providing opportunities for all children to explore the story in different ways. The range of suggested activities allows for different learning styles and preferences, recognising that children learn and respond in different ways and one size does not fit all.

It is suggested that you offer a wide variety of activities each time, so that children may choose which ones they engage with in the time given. Where time and space do not permit such a wide selection of activities to be used, try to select a few activities that offer the variety and scope for children to respond in different ways, perhaps offering different types of activity each week.

Included with the activities are suggested topics that you could talk to the children about as they participate in the activity. Ideally, an adult helper should work alongside the children at each station, to facilitate children's discussion and further learning. If this is not possible, you may wish to have an adult host at a selected number of activities and make space for independent exploration at other points.

Below you will find a short explanation of each area, and how it supports children's learning and exploration:

Small world play

In this area, you will set up a model that relates to the story, perhaps using play figures to retell the story or exploring a situation that is familiar to the children, making connections to the story.

Role play / dressing up

This activity will require a larger area, and often involves children acting out an element of the story or a scene to which they can relate, helping them to see the relationship between their own experiences and the Bible story.

Creative

These activities make use of a wide range of materials, tools and techniques. Sometimes they are collaborative, perhaps producing something to be displayed as you explore the story together. Other times, the creative activities provide children with an opportunity to make something to take home with them, as a reminder of the story.

Construction

The construction activities use a range of materials, tools and techniques to allow children to construct something, often on a larger scale, which relates to the story. These are, at times, collaborative projects, but sometimes provide children with more of a personal challenge. From time to time, the activity suggested in this area will require additional supervision and you may find it helpful to complete a risk assessment beforehand to establish safe practices.

Writing

The suggested writing activities are short, simple writing tasks, which enable children of all writing abilities to participate, responding to the story in a quieter, more reflective way.

Books

This section makes suggestions about the types of books that could be displayed for children to look at and read together, with support as needed. These may be Bible stories that retell the story, along with other books that help to provide a context for the story. Create a cosy, inviting environment, perhaps with cushions or beanbags, where children can sit together to share the stories.

Prayer and reflective activity

These activities are intended to be adult-led, providing an opportunity for prayer and reflection or discussion and questioning through a range of creative activities.

Games

Under this heading, for each session, suggestions are made about team games that can be played to support the theme of the session, or quieter board games that can be set out for children to use together.

Story time

For each session, a script is provided for telling the story in an interactive, creative way. The script may suggest props or visual aids, or may include the children in acting out parts of the story themselves.

Prayer

A short prayer is offered, focusing on what we might learn from the story, drawing the session together and giving the children the opportunity to respond in an appropriate way. You may find it helpful to introduce the prayer by saying, 'I'm going to say a prayer. Please listen carefully and, if you want to join in, you can say "Amen" at the end.'

Songs

One or two songs are suggested, which can be used each day. Some of them have actions that children can perform, while others could include dancing with ribbons or streamers or accompaniment on percussion instruments.

Take home

As you draw each session to a close, a simple idea is given for something that children can take away with them or do at home, to continue the discipling journey within the context of their own family and home.

Old Testament stories

1

God creates the world

For the team

Refer to pages 6–8 to see how the activity areas work together

Session theme

This session explores the story of creation and celebrates the great diversity in God's creation, giving children the opportunity to discover animals, birds and plants they may be unfamiliar with, and thinking about the love that God has for everything that he made.

Bible text: Genesis 1—2

Team prayer

Creator God, thank you for the beautiful world that you created, which we can explore and enjoy. Thank you for your great diversity in creation, that there is always something new for us to discover. Help us to share the great joy of creation with the children with whom we work. Amen

Activity areas

Small world play

Provide a tuff spot (builder's tray), small world play trees and plants and a selection of animal figures, along with a man and a woman figurine. Work together with the children to add each element in order to create the garden of Eden.

Talk about the way that God added something new each day which came together to create our beautiful world. What would the world be like if any element was missing? What do we need to do to take care of the world?

Role play / dressing up

Provide a selection of appropriate dressing-up items and props which children can use to role play being a gardener. These could include wellington boots, aprons, gardening gloves, plant pots, trowels and watering cans.

Talk about Adam and Eve's life in the garden of Eden when God had first created the world. If everything was perfect in the world that God created, would there have been weeds growing? Would Adam and Eve have had any jobs to do? What would they do all day?

Creative

Before the session, cut large numbers 1–7 from thick paper or card. Gather a selection of collage materials, including magazines, catalogues, used wrapping paper, stickers, feathers and so on, and make these available, along with scissors and glue. Invite the children to collage each of the numbers to represent the things that God created or did on that day, covering each number with the appropriate images.

Talk about the huge variety seen on each day; our world is so bright and colourful thanks to God's great creativity!

Construction

Gather a selection of junk modelling materials and provide scissors, glue, sticky tape, and so on. Challenge the children to see what they can create from the provided 'junk' that would normally be thrown away, giving a completely free choice about what they make.

Talk about the different ways that we can reuse the junk materials to make something new. God wants us to take care of his created world. How can we make better use of the resources that we have and take responsibility for the environment?

Writing

Print out some pictures of rare or unusual animals or birds, which the children may be unfamiliar with, and invite them to name the animals, thinking imaginatively and writing their dreamt-up names on a label for each animal.

Talk about the way that God asked Adam to name each of the animals. How do you think he decided upon each of their names? How long do you think it took him?

Books

Provide books telling the creation story, along with age-appropriate children's Bibles. You could also offer books about people, including books about different people groups or tribes and books about animals, birds, plants, oceans and space.

Talk about the things which interest the children when they look at the books. Some children will be happy to read independently, while others may need support with reading. Support them as needed, in a low-key way so as to include all children interested in this activity, regardless of reading ability.

Prayer and reflective activity

Provide paper and paint and invite the children to paint a picture to show their favourite part of God's creation, whether it's an animal or bird, plant or landscape; allow free choice here and encourage the children to think creatively. Create a display of the children's paintings with the heading: Thank you, God, for...

Talk about the different things that the children choose to include in their pictures and why they like each of these particular things. Explain that God wanted us to enjoy his beautiful world.

Story time

Today's story is told through the use of the collaged numbers which the children will have created during the session. Before you begin the story, you could also invite the children to prepare appropriate actions or sound effects to add for each day. With a larger group, divide the children into seven small groups and assign one day to each group; smaller groups of children can participate in each and every day.

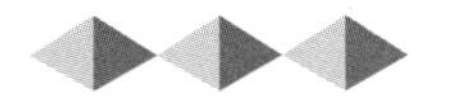

This morning we have been exploring the story of creation, thinking about the beautiful world that God created and how we should take responsibility to look after it. This story is told in the first book of the Bible, in Genesis.

A very long time ago, before the world was made, there was nothing but God. God spoke the world into existence, creating all the things that we enjoy today.

On the first day *(invite a child to hold up the number 1)* God said, 'Let there be light,' and light appeared in the sky. God had created day and night and he was pleased with what he had done.

On the second day *(invite a child to hold up the number 2)* God spoke again. He said, 'Sky' and 'Sea,' and the waters divided, forming the sea below and the sky above. God looked at what he had made and he was happy.

On the third day *(invite a child to hold up the number 3)* God said, 'Let the waters on earth come together, and let's have some dry land, where plants and trees and beautiful flowers can grow.' So God created the land and the seas and he was happy with his work.

On the fourth day *(invite a child to hold up the number 4)* God spoke again, 'We need lights in the sky to mark the day and the night.' In the daytime, a beautiful ball of shining warm light appeared in the sky, the sun, and at night, the gentle cool moon appeared, surrounded by twinkling stars all around. God looked at what he had done and was happy with his work.

On the fifth day *(invite a child to hold up the number 5)* God spoke again, 'Flying things in the sky, and swimming things in the sea.' As he said this, the sky was filled with birds, and butterflies of every colour, wings flapping and dancing in the air. The sea below was filled with shiny, silvery fish which slithered and swam through the waters. God looked at his work and was happy.

On the sixth day *(invite a child to hold up the number 6)* God said, 'Let animals walk on the land, stomping and slithering, crawling and galloping,' and animals of every type filled the earth. Then God said, 'Let us make human beings, to walk on the earth and care for this beautiful creation.' God looked at his beautiful world and was very happy with all that he had made.

On the seventh day *(invite a child to hold up the number 7)* God took a rest and enjoyed his beautiful world.

Prayer

Father God, thank you for the beautiful world that you created. We thank you especially for... (invite the children to call out some of the things they may want to thank God for). Amen

Songs

Songs today could include:

- 'He's got the whole world in his hands' (Anon)
- 'What a great creator' (John Hardwick)

Take home

Suggest that together with their families, the children could start to make a 'creation scrapbook', gathering photos, pictures and found items such as feathers, pressed flowers, and so on, and talk about the things they enjoy most in God's beautiful world.

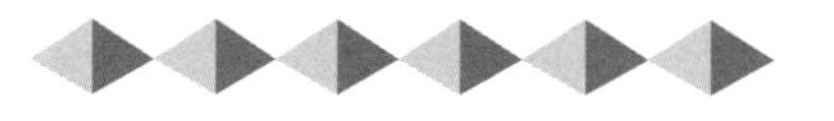

2

Adam and Eve make a bad choice

For the team

Refer to pages 6–8 to see how the activity areas work together

Session theme

Today's session explores the way that God's perfect creation was spoiled when Adam and Eve made a bad choice. Through this session, children have the opportunity to think about the choices we make, while recognising that God's love for us does not change, no matter how we act.

Bible text: Genesis 3

Team prayer

Dear God, thank you for the gift of free choice. We are sorry for the times when we make bad choices, doing things that we know would not please you. Help us to share, honestly, with the children we work with that you always love us, and give us the chance to start again. Amen

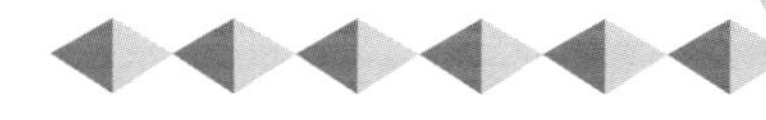

Activity areas

Small world play

Reintroduce the garden of Eden in the tuff spot you had in the previous session, with trees and plants, a selection of animal figures, and a man and a woman figurine. Include a snake in the scene and a tree right in the middle of the garden.

Talk about what children know about the story and help them to retell what happened to Adam and Eve when they met the serpent.

Role play / dressing up

Set up a work environment, such as a building site or garden scene, where children can pretend to engage in physical work. You could ask one of your helpers to oversee this activity and exaggerate the need for the children to work hard, perhaps giving orders to them as the workers.

Talk about the way that Adam and Eve enjoyed their time in the garden, but after they had made their bad choice, they then had to work hard for the things that they had and their freedom was gone.

Creative

Provide a selection of different fruits, including some which will be new to the children, as well as more familiar fruit pieces. You will also need small bowls, sharp knives (to be used by an adult or under close supervision, as appropriate) and a chopping board and spoons. Invite the children to work with you to create a fruit salad, chopping up the larger pieces of fruit, under supervision, and mixing the pieces of fruit in the small bowls. Encourage the children to try the different fruits, particularly those they may never have tried before.

Talk about the children's favourite types of fruit and what they think about the new fruits they are trying. God told Adam and Eve there was only one fruit in the garden which they shouldn't eat, but they broke his rule and disobeyed him.

Construction

Gather a selection of twigs which have an interesting shape. If possible, take the children outside to do this. Provide modelling clay in the appropriate colours and invite the children to select a twig to use as a tree trunk, before using the modelling clay to add leaves and fruit shapes on to the branches to construct a small model tree.

Talk about how it seems so easy for Adam and Eve to follow this one rule, not to eat fruit from that particular tree, but they still broke the rule. Do we find it easy to follow rules?

Books

Set out the same books that you had out in the previous session, with a selection of age-appropriate children's Bibles and creation story books so that children can make the connection with the previous part of the story and see the continuity.

Support the children in reading the books, where necessary, and discuss with them the things that interest them.

Prayer and reflective activity

Set out a large bin and provide paper and pens. Invite the children to write or draw something that they want to say sorry to God for on one of the pieces of paper, before screwing the paper up and throwing it into the bin.

Talk about what it means to say sorry to God for the things that we do wrong. He takes the rubbish that we do and deals with it so that we don't have to worry about it any more. Talk sensitively about any specific issues that this activity raises for the children.

Games

The board game Snakes and Ladders would be a good choice for today. There are large garden editions of the game available which would work well, if space allows.

Story time

Invite the children to sit down with you, giving each of them a small lump of playdough, which they will need to use as you retell the story. Explain that as the story unfolds, you will ask them to make a number of different models from the playdough. As they create each one in turn, they can reuse the same lump of playdough.

Last week we heard how God created this beautiful world, with plants and trees, birds and fish, animals and humans. When God had finished creating this beautiful place, he enjoyed spending time with Adam and Eve, watching them enjoying all that he had made. He gave them only one rule.

Ask the children to make Adam or Eve.

He showed them the tree in the middle of the garden, and told them that they could eat the fruit that grew on any tree, apart from that one tree. God told them that this tree would let them understand things that only God should know, and for that reason they should leave the tree alone.

Ask the children to make a model of a tree.

One day, when Eve was walking through the garden, she saw a snake.

Ask the children to make a model of a snake.

The snake tricked Eve, telling her that God should let them eat the fruit, and it would be fine if they ate some.

Ask the children to make the shape of a piece of fruit.

Eve listened to the snake. She ate the fruit and she persuaded Adam to do the same!

Straight away, things changed for Adam and Eve. They knew that they had done something wrong and they tried to hide from God.

God looked at his beautiful world.

Ask the children to make a model of one of their favourite things in creation, and invite one or two children to share their models, as time allows.

Now that Adam and Eve had broken God's only rule, things would never be the same again. God told Adam and Eve that from now on, they would need to work hard and would not be able to enjoy his beautiful garden in the same way again.

God's beautiful world, and his relationship with Adam and Eve, was spoiled.

Ask the children to squash their models flat.

Prayer

Father God, we're sorry for the way we break rules, like Adam and Eve did, and don't always listen to the things that you tell us. Thank you that you give us a brand new chance to start again, and that we can still be your friends. Amen

Songs

Songs today could include:

- 'I can do all things' (Jim Bailey)
- 'If I've been wrong' (Sammy Horner)

Take home

You could suggest that the children in your group spend some time talking to their families about the times when they have difficult choices to make about how they should behave or act, or when they feel under pressure to act wrongly, and to talk about how they can handle these situations.

3

Noah and the ark

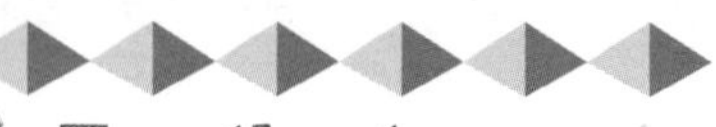

For the team

Refer to pages 6–8 to see how the activity areas work together

Session theme

Through this session, we explore one of the most well-known Bible stories, which the children will probably be very familiar with, but rather than focusing on the familiar themes of animals, boats and bad weather, this session also looks at the idea that God had to give the world a brand new start, and how he promised never to flood the earth again.

Bible text: Genesis 6—9

Team prayer

Father God, as we share this story with the children today, help us not to dwell upon sentimental images of smiling animals aboard a boat, but to bring to life the reality that you give a fresh start to everyone who accepts the invitation. Amen

Activity areas

Small world play

Set up a water tray and provide a number of different containers which will float on the water. Provide a number of small plastic animals and challenge the children to predict which container will hold the most animals, while remaining afloat. The children can then explore with the animals to discover the answer for themselves.

Talk about the way that God gave Noah precise instructions for building the ark, which Noah followed to make sure that all the animals stayed safe.

Creative

Prepare a large rainbow outline on a large sheet of paper and provide a selection of different collaging resources in a variety of colours, textures and materials. Provide PVA glue and invite the children to help you to complete the rainbow by sticking small pieces of the different materials into the appropriate colour section of the image you have drawn.

Talk about the children's own experiences of seeing rainbows in the sky and how they still remind us today that God always keeps his promises.

Construction

Invite the children to help 'build the ark'. Softwoods work best for this activity and activities will need to be completed under close supervision, once the appropriate risk assessments have been completed. This activity could either focus on the different ways that we work with wood, such as sandpapering wood to make it smooth, hammering nails into wood, putting screws into the wood (once started off for children), and even sawing wood held in a vice, or children could be offered pieces of wood in different shapes and sizes to put together to make their own small toy ark.

Talk about the things you can make with wood and what you have to do to the wood as you work with it. How hard did Noah have to work to build his ark?

Writing

Stick pieces of paper up around the room, each headed with a different letter of the alphabet. Invite the children to write animal names beginning with each letter on the appropriate sheet and challenge them to find one for every letter of the alphabet.

Talk about the children's favourite animals. Which ones would they like to care for? Which ones would they rather not go near?

Books

Provide a selection of children's Bibles and story books which retell the story of Noah and the ark. You could also display a selection of books about animals, particularly those which talk about how we care for animals.

Support the children in reading the books, where necessary, and discuss with them the things that interest them.

Prayer and reflective activity

This activity could be done at a window, or by using a sheet of clear plastic. If it isn't actually raining, use a water spray bottle to spray a number of drops at the top of the window or plastic sheet. Invite the children to choose and trace one of the 'raindrops' as it runs down the window and, as they do so, to say sorry to God for something they may have done.

Talk about the way that God used the flood to give the world a fresh, brand new start and he will do the same for us too, when we say sorry to him. Talk about any particular issues that this raises for the children.

Games

There are a large number of Noah's ark toys, games or jigsaw puzzles available to purchase which would work well for this session. Alternatively, provide pairs of small animal figures for children to play with, along with a cardboard box that you could make into a basic ark shape.

Story time

This story is told with the children participating by adding their own sound effects to the story. Ask the children to sit down with you, explain the sound effects as detailed in the script below, and encourage the children to join in at the appropriate moments.

God was very sad. He looked around the beautiful world that he had made and all he could see was people hurting one another, being unkind and unloving. He searched high and low to find anyone who was still following God and doing the right things. Eventually, he found one man, Noah, and his family who were still following God and living their lives in a good way. So God came up with a plan. It was a sad and difficult plan, but it would mean that God could give the world a brand new, fresh start, so that his people could start again.

God told Noah to build a really big boat—an ark.

Ask the children to mime hammering nails into wood, with appropriate banging sounds.

When the people around him saw what he was doing, they laughed at Noah.

Ask the children to laugh.

There was no water anywhere near to the place where Noah was building his boat. But Noah carried on building. He knew he was doing the right thing because it was what God had told him to do.

Children continue to mime hammering, as before.

When the boat was ready, God told Noah to bring two of every kind of animal on to the ark. What animals do you think there were?

Ask the children to think of different types of animals and to perform the different animal noises, as appropriate.

And when Noah, his family and all the animals were safely on board, God shut the door.

Children can give a loud clap.

Then, the rain began to trickle down, just a little at first *(ask the children to lightly tap their thighs with their fingertips)*, then more, and more.

Encourage the children to tap harder and harder, building up the sound as they do so.

It rained and rained for 40 days and 40 nights and the waters rose high above the trees and houses, high above the hills and mountains. Eventually the rain stopped, but it would take many days of waiting for the sun to dry up all the rain. Noah, his family and the animals waited safely on board the ark.

Eventually, the waters dried up. Noah and his family were finally able to put their feet back on dry land. The animals left the ark and made new homes for themselves and God's world was given a brand new, fresh start.

Encourage the children to cheer.

God did one more thing: he painted the first rainbow in the sky as a sign of his promise that he would never again flood the whole earth. So when we see a rainbow in the sky, we can remember that promise too.

Prayer

Father God, we are sorry for the times when we hurt other people and don't do the things that you would expect us to do. Thank you that you give us a fresh start, just as you gave the world a fresh start in today's story. Thank you too for rainbows; a beautiful reminder that you always keep your promises. Amen

Songs

Songs today could include:

- 'Rainbow' (David and Beci Wakerly)

Take home

Suggest that the children create their own picture of a rainbow this week, as well as keeping their eyes peeled just in case they spot one.

God's promise to Abraham and Sarah

For the team

Refer to pages 6–8 to see how the activity areas work together

Session theme

There are many stories involving Abraham, Sarah and Isaac, but this session focuses on the promise that God made to Abraham, that he would have a son, and the way God fulfilled this promise with the birth of Isaac.

Bible text: Genesis 15; 17:1—18:15; 21:1–7

Team prayer

Father God, just as Abraham and Sarah had to wait many, many years until Isaac arrived, help us to trust in you, even when we have to wait for the future that you have planned for us. Amen

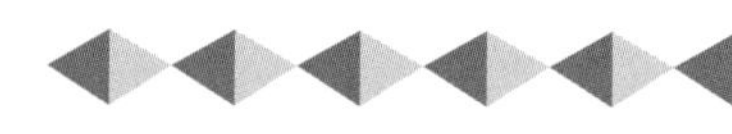

Activity areas

Role play / dressing up

Gather a number of different dolls as well as things you may need to take care of a baby, such as doll's clothes, nappies, toy bottles, blankets, a cot or toy pram and perhaps a baby bath, etc., for the children to use to role play caring for a baby.

Talk about the children's experiences of caring for a baby, perhaps a sibling or cousin. Can they imagine what it would have been like for Abraham and Sarah to suddenly have a baby when they were already older than the children's grandparents are?

Creative

Provide pieces of black sugar paper, along with coloured sand and PVA glue, and encourage the children to come and create their own sand art picture or pattern, by sprinkling coloured sand over the glue which they have spread on to the paper.

Talk about God's promise that Abraham would have more descendants than there are grains of sand on the seashore. We can't even count the grains of sand on our pictures; how many more grains of sand must there be on the beach?

Construction

Collect a variety of items that can be used as a tent frame, such as laundry dryers, poles, tables and chairs along with blankets and sheets to build some tents together. Let the children take a lead in the construction process, checking for stability as appropriate.

Talk about children's experiences of spending a night in a tent. Can they imagine what it would be like to live in a tent all the time? (Explain that the climate in the land where Abraham and Sarah lived was quite different from our own!)

Writing

Provide strips of card, along with coloured pens and pencils, and invite the children to create a name plaque, drawing their name in a fancy style and decorating it as they wish.

Talk about what the children's names mean, perhaps looking them up in a baby name book as needed. Explain that the name Isaac means 'laughter', and was the name which God told Abraham to give to his son.

Books

Alongside the children's Bibles and story books which tell the story of Abraham and Sarah, you could also provide a selection of books which tell some of the other stories of Abraham and Isaac as well as other stories about new babies.

Read the stories to the children if they wish, or discuss the stories as the children look at them.

Prayer and reflective activity

Give each child a small plastic bottle and provide different coloured sands for the children to use to fill their bottles with layers of different colours.

Talk about some of the different things that God promises for us, as the children fill the bottles with different layers of sand, and how God always hears our prayers and keeps his promises to us, even when we have to wait a long time, as Abraham did.

Games

Hide a number of small stars, either glow-in-the-dark or stars cut from shiny card, around the room before the session. Invite the children to hunt for the stars, either counting the stars that they can see, or working together to gather the stars as a group and then count them.

Talk about how many stars you can see in the sky on a really dark night. God promised Abraham he would have more descendants than there are stars in the sky.

Story time

Today's retelling is performed by two adults, playing the roles of Abraham and Sarah. It would work well if they were in appropriate costume and could learn the script in advance of the session so that they can stand in front of the children and tell the story, as though they were just talking to them about what they had experienced. They will need a doll, wrapped in a blanket, to hold.

Sarah: Hello everyone, my name is Sarah and this is my husband, Abraham. We want to tell you what happened to us. I don't think you'll believe our story!

Abraham: No, that's right! It's a very surprising story. It all began a very long time ago. I was talking to God one night, thanking him for all the things that he had done for us, but there was one thing missing. We had no children of our own, and we really wanted to

	have our own family. God said something very surprising. He told me to look at all the stars in the sky; one day, he said, there would be more people in my family than there were stars in the sky! Then he told me to look at all the grains of sand under my feet. He said we would have more people in our family than all the grains of sand along the seashore! What a strange thing to say!
Sarah:	It was a very strange thing. I'm not sure I believed you, Abraham. After all, we waited such a long time to have a baby, and nothing happened.
Abraham:	Then, one day, three men came visiting; do you remember, Sarah?
Sarah:	How could I forget? We don't get many visitors and here we had three men on their travels who needed taking care of.
Abraham:	That's right. You cooked them a meal, didn't you? And I sat down to talk to them. They said the strangest thing. They told me that they would come back in a year's time, and by then, Sarah would have had a baby boy!
Sarah:	Well, I just laughed! I'm too old to have a baby, I thought. All my friends are grandmas now, great-grandmas even!
Abraham:	It did seem very silly, but that was a whole year ago now, and look. Sure enough, Sarah had a baby boy, just as the visitors said.
Sarah:	We called him Isaac, just as God told Abraham so many years ago. It means laughter.
Abraham:	Ooh, Sarah, I can hear some voices. I think we have visitors. I wonder who that could be...

Abraham and Sarah leave the scene together.

Prayer

Father God, thank you for the promise that you made to Abraham and Sarah. Thank you that you always keep your promises and we can trust the things you say and do. Amen

Songs

Songs today could include:

- 'Father Abraham had many sons' (Anon)

Take home

Give each child a glow-in-the-dark star to take home with them as a reminder of today's story and the way that God keeps his promises to us, just as he did for Abraham and Sarah, even when they had to wait a long time. Also, encourage them to take their bottles of coloured sand home with them as a further reminder.

5

Joseph is taken to Egypt

For the team

Refer to pages 6–8 to see how the activity areas work together

Session theme

This is the first of a two-part series exploring the life of Joseph. In this session, we discover more about Joseph's relationships with his family, and how this led to his departure to Egypt, providing an opportunity to think about our own family relationships.

Bible text: Genesis 37

Team prayer

Father God, thank you for the stories of heroes in the Bible and the lessons that we can learn from them, both the times when they were serving you well and the times when, like us, they made mistakes and got things wrong. Help us to share this message with the children we work with today. Amen

Activity areas

Small world play

Set up a shallow sand tray with a sandy base and provide a selection of play figure people, camels and sheep. At one end of the scene, provide some pyramids (these could be made from sandpaper) to indicate Egypt. Invite the children to retell the story of Joseph taking food to his brothers, before being sold into slavery and taken to Egypt.

Talk about what happened in the story and how Joseph must have felt. God was looking after Joseph even when he was in this low place.

Role play / dressing up

Gather a selection of different dressing-up outfits in a variety of different styles. Invite the children to try them on, perhaps parading them around.

Talk about how the children feel about the different clothes. Which are their favourites? Which ones make them feel special? Why? How do you think Joseph felt when his father gave him his coat? How did his brothers feel?

Creative

Gather a selection of fabric scraps including felt and fabrics in a variety of colours and textures. You will also need scissors, glue, needles and thread and could offer fabric pens or paints too. Invite the children to come and create and decorate their own colourful coat for a teddy bear. (You could have a number of teddy bears available to help the children with sizing.) Help the children to cut out a basic sleeveless jacket shape, before sewing or glueing other colourful pieces of fabric to the base, or decorating with the fabric paints or pens.

Talk about the care that Jacob took in having the colourful coat made for Joseph; it was a special gift to show how much he loved his son.

Writing

Provide some illustrations or images of different scenes from today's story, along with speech and thought-bubble sticky notes. Invite the children to choose a character that stands out to them on one of the pictures, and to write what they think that person may be thinking or feeling at that point.

Talk about how many different thoughts and feelings appear in this story. God always knows how we are thinking and feeling and cares about us at all of these times, whether we are happy or sad.

Books

Display a selection of children's Bibles and books which tell some of the stories of Joseph's life. Other books offered today could include stories about different families.

Support the children in reading the books, where necessary, and discuss with them the things that interest them.

Prayer and reflective activity

Provide paper and watercolour paints and invite the children to paint their own family portrait, including all the people who are special to them.

Talk about Joseph and how he didn't always have a good relationship with his family. Encourage the children to pray for their families as they complete their paintings, and help them to think about the different things that they can pray about.

Games

Games played today could include the card game Happy Families, where children have to collect a full suit of family members by swapping cards with other players. Alternatively, you could play a more active version of the game, where the children have a character name written on a label and attached to their back, and have to ask the other children a series of 'yes/no' questions to discover their identity before finding the other members of their family.

Story time

Today's story retelling will require a number of volunteers; for smaller groups you may be able to include everyone in acting out the story. You will also need a brightly coloured jacket or cardigan to use as the coat which Jacob gave to Joseph. Assign the roles of Joseph, Jacob, the brothers and the Ishmaelites to different children, ready to help as you retell the story.

Last week we heard how God gave baby Isaac to Abraham and Sarah. When Isaac grew up, he had a son called Jacob, and when Jacob grew up, he had twelve sons.

Bring Jacob and the twelve brothers into the middle of the group.

Like most families, Jacob's sons didn't always get along together. Sometimes they fought and argued. Jacob's favourite son was Joseph, and this made his brothers very jealous.

Encourage the other brothers to interact with Joseph appropriately.

And Joseph didn't always help matters. He often told tales to his dad about the things his brothers had got up to. Then he had some strange dreams. In one dream, Joseph saw bundles of wheat, gathered together by himself and his brothers. In his dream, all his brothers' bundles of wheat bowed down to his bundle! Then he had another dream where he saw the sun, moon and eleven stars bowing down to him too! Now even his dad, who loved him very much, thought he was showing off.

But Jacob still loved Joseph very much indeed. One day, he gave him a special gift—a fancy coat which he had made for his son, so much more luxurious and expensive than anything any of his brothers owned. Joseph was delighted!

As Jacob puts the coat on Joseph, he could parade up and down, showing it off.

One day, Jacob sent Joseph off to the fields where his brothers were working. The brothers saw this as their chance to teach Joseph a lesson. They jumped on him, tore off his coat and threw him into a deep well.

Encourage the children to mime this, safely.

At first, they wanted to kill their brother, but then they saw some travelling Ishmaelites, heading to Egypt. The brothers saw this as their chance to get rid of their annoying show-off of a brother, and get some money too! So they sold him as a slave to the Ishmaelites who took Joseph with them on their way.

Send the Ishmaelites 'off stage', together with Joseph.

The brothers lied to their dad about what had happened to Joseph, taking home his precious coat covered in the blood of a goat, and telling Jacob that Joseph had been killed! Jacob was devastated; the son he loved so much was gone.

The brothers should bring the coat back to Jacob.

So Joseph found himself separated from his family. One day, they would be reunited again. But Joseph would have a lifetime of adventures first.

Prayer

Dear God, thank you for our families, big and small. Thank you for the fun times that we spend together and for the way they love and care for us. We're sorry for the times when we argue, like Joseph and his brothers. Please help us to learn how to show love and forgiveness in our families. Amen

Songs

Songs today could include:

- 'Big family of God' (Becky Drake)
- 'Our God is a great big God' (Nigel and Jo Hemming)

Take home

Suggest to the children that they could plan one positive surprise for someone in their family, this week, to show them how much they matter to them, and how much they are loved.

Joseph serves God

For the team

Refer to pages 6–8 to see how the activity areas work together

Session theme

This is the second of two sessions exploring the life of Joseph, in which we see the way God lifted him out from his time in jail, to a life of power and authority serving under Pharaoh. This session considers the way that we, like Joseph, can serve God in every situation in which we find ourselves.

Bible text: Genesis 39—45

Team prayer

Father God, thank you that we have the opportunity to serve you, as we work with these children. Help us to remember that whether we find ourselves in the lowliest position or given places of authority, we serve you first and foremost. Amen

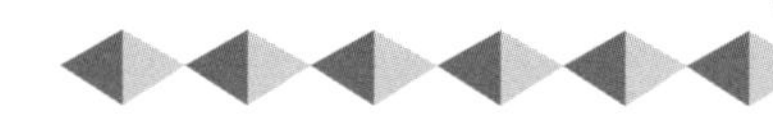

Activity areas

Small world play

Set up the sand tray as in the previous session, with pyramids to indicate Egypt as a setting. Invite the children to use building blocks or bricks to build a prison at one end of the scene and a palace at the other.

Talk about the way that God brought Joseph from the lowest place, to the highest. God is with us in every circumstance, just as he was with Joseph.

Role play / dressing up

Provide clipboards with paper and pens, along with different numbers of objects, perhaps in sacks, for counting. Show the children how to use a tally chart to record how many of each thing there are.

Talk about the way that Joseph was given responsibility for overseeing how much grain was stored, to make sure that there was enough for the years of famine.

Creative

Provide a selection of different beads, including some which are gold in colour, and lengths of cord and invite the children to thread their own necklaces. There is also scope for other jewellery-making activities here, such as Egyptian headdresses cut from card and painted in metallic colours, and ring-making too.

Talk about the way that Pharaoh gave Joseph a necklace and gold ring, as well as new clothes, as a sign of the special role that he had given him. How do we feel when someone gives us something special?

Construction

Gather a number of cardboard boxes and work together to use some of these boxes to build storehouses where the grain could be stored.

Talk about Joseph and how he knew what the Egyptians would need to do to survive the years of famine. Joseph listened to God and did as he told him.

Books

Offer a variety of age-appropriate children's Bibles and story books about Joseph alongside a selection of non-fiction books about Ancient Egypt for the children to look at and share together. You could also provide a selection of holiday brochures for Egypt for the children to look at and think about how the country has changed since Joseph's day.

Talk about the things the children notice from the illustrations in the books and offer to read the books to the children if they wish.

Prayer and reflective activity

Set out a large sheet of paper and pens and invite the children to add their own ideas about how God speaks to us, by writing or drawing them on the paper.

Talk about the way that Joseph heard from God through the dreams that he had and was able to interpret for other people. Talk about the children's own thoughts about how God speaks to us today.

Games

Today, you could play a selection of team games, where the children have to collect things together, perhaps searching around the room for counters of a particular colour, for instance, as a reminder of the way that Joseph and his family were brought back together.

Story time

As you tell the story today, invite the children to use some of the things that they have made as they play the different roles. Some children can keep a tally of the grain, others can wear the Egyptian headdresses as Pharaoh and others can use the storehouses to gather the grain together.

While he was in Egypt, Joseph found himself in a very difficult situation and ended up in jail! While he was there, he continued to tell people what their dreams meant, listening to what God told him.

One day he even had the chance to tell two of Pharaoh's servants what their dreams meant, and much later, one of those men had the chance to tell Pharaoh all about Joseph; it was his chance to get out of jail!

Joseph found himself in the palace of the Pharaoh, helping him to understand that God was talking to him through his dreams too. God was warning Pharaoh that they would have seven good harvest years, but after that there would be seven very difficult years.

Joseph helped Pharaoh to plan for these years of famine, advising him how to store food away so the people would not go hungry. Pharaoh made Joseph his second in command, helping him to rule over all the people.

When the famine years began, there was plenty of food in the storehouses, so much that people travelled from miles away to ask for food when they had none. Some of the people who came to Egypt were Joseph's brothers! They had no idea that Joseph would still be alive even, and didn't recognise him at first.

Joseph wanted to make sure that the brothers had learned their lesson and watched to see how they cared for their youngest brother. When he saw that they had changed their ways, he revealed himself to them, told them that he forgave them, and the whole family were reunited, safe from the famine in Egypt.

Prayer

Thank you, Father God, that no matter where we go, or what we do, you will always be with us. Help us to show other people what it means to be a follower of God, as Joseph did, wherever we find ourselves. Amen

Songs

Songs today could include:

- 'When you're somewhere strange and new' (Steve Morgan-Gurr)

Take home

Suggest to the children that they spend some time talking to their families about all the different places they go to: school, work, clubs, etc. What does it mean for them to take God with them into those places?

7

The baby in the basket

For the team

Refer to pages 6–8 to see how the activity areas work together

Session theme

This is the first in a series of three sessions, exploring some key events in the life of Moses, remembering that God had his hand on Moses, and was protecting him right from the start.

Bible text: Exodus 2:1–10

Team prayer

Father God, thank you that you used this tiny baby to change the course of history, and that you watch over each of us too, protecting us from harm. Amen

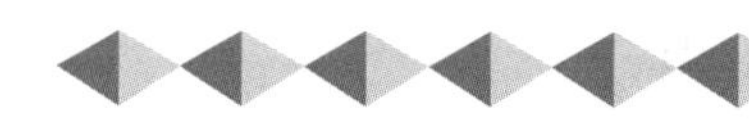

Activity areas

Small world play

Put stoppers at each end of a half drainpipe, with sand in the base and reeds along the edge, before filling with water to create a river. Provide small amounts of modelling clay for the children to use to mould and sculpt baskets, which they can then experiment with to find a basket shape that can float on the water.

Moses' mother took time creating a basket, before painting it with pitch to make sure that it was waterproof and would float safely.

Role play / dressing up

Provide a number of baby dolls along with some of the equipment they may need to be taken care of, such as prams, pushchairs, cribs, small nappies and wet wipes, baby clothes, blankets and disused baby bottles. Encourage the children to take care of the babies, changing, feeding and cuddling them as needed.

Talk about children's own experiences of helping to take care of a baby and the different things that we need to do to take care of a baby.

Creative

Offer some small baskets to be woven. For this activity, small basket weaving kits can be purchased, which include a card frame and raffia. Alternatively, paper bowls can be used to create a frame. Make vertical cuts around the side of the bowl at equal intervals, then weave strips of paper in and out, so that it looks like a woven basket.

Talk about the way that Moses' mother carefully wove the basket ready to keep her baby safe.

Construction

Provide wooden building blocks and invite the children to help to build some pyramids. This activity could be done collaboratively or you could hold a little competition to see who can build the best pyramid.

Talk about the slaves and how they would have had a very different experience of building the pyramids. It would not have been fun for them!

Writing

Provide some copies of the Egyptian hieroglyph alphabet, along with strips of paper and pencils. Invite the children to 'write' their own name in hieroglyphs. Not all the letters of our alphabet have a corresponding hieroglyph, so children will need to see how many letters they can actually write or draw.

Talk about the way that the different letters are represented. Not everyone would have been able to read or write, only those in positions of authority over the slaves.

Books

Offer a selection of age-appropriate non-fiction books about Egypt, rivers and babies along with children's Bibles and story books about Moses.

Support the children in reading the books, where necessary, and discuss with them the things that interest them.

Prayer and reflective activity

Cut out some simple flower shapes from paper and provide a bowl of water and pencils. Invite the children to write the name of, or draw a family member, who they wish to pray for, on one of the flowers, before folding down the petals and placing into the flower. Encourage the children to watch as the petals unfurl and pray for their family member as they do so.

Talk about the way that Moses' mother would have prayed for him as she had to say goodbye to him. We can pray for our family too, that God would bless and protect them.

Story time

Today's story retelling takes place around the drainpipe river, used for the small world play activity. Invite the children to sit on the floor with you, around the river, ready to listen to the story.

A long time after Joseph had been in Egypt, there were many, many of God's people living in the country, but the Pharaoh had forgotten Joseph and what he had done for Egypt. The Pharaohs now treated God's people very badly. They were kept as slaves, working very hard for very little money.

Then, one day, the Pharaoh decided that God's people were becoming too great in number, and he was worried that they might start causing problems, so he issued a very cruel decree. Any baby boys born to the Israelites would have to be killed!

It was while all this was taking place that a young Israelite woman had a baby boy who she loved very much. To begin with, she hid her baby boy in her home so that the Egyptian guards could not hurt him. But as the baby grew older, his mother knew she would have to do something different to keep him safe. So, she came up with a plan.

First she wove a basket from reeds that she collected, then she painted it with pitch to waterproof the basket. She took her baby into her arms, gave him a big cuddle, kissed him and prayed for him, that God would keep him safe. She put him into the basket, and carried the basket down to the River Nile, where she gently floated the basket in the water.

Use the props that the children have been playing with in the 'Small world play' area to re-enact this part of the story.

The baby's mother asked his older sister to hide in the reeds and wait until someone found him. It wasn't long before someone did come by—a princess, the daughter of the Pharaoh, who had come down to the river to bathe. She saw the baby in the basket, and quickly scooped him up in her arms.

'What a beautiful baby! I wonder whose baby he is,' said the princess, 'I will call him Moses. We must take care of him.'

Then the baby's sister appeared out of the reeds. She offered to find someone to take care of the baby for the princess. And who do you think she went to find?

Moses' mother, of course! Moses was raised by his own mum and family, for the princess who made sure that nobody harmed him. All that time, God was looking after Moses.

Prayer

Father God, thank you that Moses' mother trusted you to take care of her son, and you did. Thank you that you care for the people who matter to us too. Amen

Songs

Songs today could include:

- 'Our God is a great big God' (Nigel and Jo Hemming)

Take home

Encourage the children, when they get home, to talk about the different ways that God has cared for their families in the different situations they have been through. You could suggest that they spend some time praying as a family to thank God for his care.

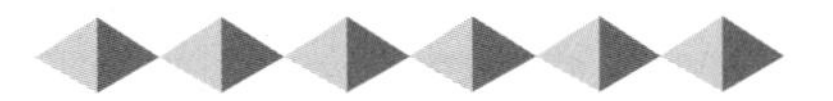

8 Escape from Egypt

For the team

Refer to pages 6–8 to see how the activity areas work together

Session theme

This is the second in a series of three sessions exploring the life of Moses. Today's epic tale explores the plagues inflicted on Egypt to persuade the Pharaoh to let God's people go, and how the Israelites were brought safely out of Egypt and across the Red Sea.

Bible text: Exodus 5—14

Team prayer

Father God, thank you for your great gift of freedom. Help us to communicate this message in a way that children will understand, and celebrate the freedom that you have given each of us. Amen

Activity areas

Small world play

Set out a tray with recognisable Egyptian scenery—a base layer of sand, a channel filled with water to represent the river, some pyramid shapes (which could be made from card and covered with sandpaper) and some camel toys. One by one, provide small props relating to some of the plagues of Egypt, including as many as you find appropriate to your children. These could include adding a drop of red food colouring to the river, toy frogs and insects, small ice cubes as hail and a piece of black fabric to spread over the top of the scene.

Talk about each of the plagues as you add them to the scene. Why do you think God had to send each of these plagues to Egypt?

Role play / dressing up

Provide a variety of toy vehicles for the children to play with: these could include hobby horses, bikes, scooters, go-karts, etc., in a large playing area.

Talk about the different ways that we travel, including larger vehicles. The Israelites had none of these means available to them and had to move fast when they were set free from Egypt, before the Pharaoh changed his mind and sent his armies to chase the Israelites in chariots.

Creative

Set out a length of lining paper, provide paint and brushes and work together with the children to create a mural scene of the crossing of the Red Sea. You could either prepare an outline drawing for the children to fill in with paint, or work together to decide upon the design and details to include.

Talk about what it must have been like to actually be there in the scene, when the Israelites crossed the Red Sea. This scene has been created in many paintings and films, but we can only really imagine what it would have been like to be there.

Construction

Create some mud bricks with the children from soil which is rich in clay, added to straw, sand and water. Experiment with different amounts of each component, before mixing together and leaving to set in small plastic containers.

Talk about how hard the slaves had to work to create the bricks for the Egyptians. When Aaron and Moses asked Pharaoh to let the Israelites leave, he refused and made their work harder for them by forcing the slaves to find their own straw to add to the brick mixture.

Books

Along with a selection of children's Bibles and story books about Moses and the exodus story, provide a number of non-fiction books about Egypt, particularly those which include information about how slaves were used to build pyramids and other buildings.

Support the children in reading the books, where necessary, and discuss with them the things that interest them.

Prayer and reflective activity

Provide a few helium balloons and ask the children to think about what kinds of things God wants to set us free from. Write these on the balloons with a marker pen, before setting the balloon free as a symbol of the freedom God has given to us.

Talk about children's own ideas for the things that hold us down. Why does God want to set us free from these things? How can we live differently when we accept his gift of freedom?

Games

Games played today could include chasing and setting-free games such as stuck-in-the-mud, to remind the children of the way that God set his people free from slavery.

Story time

This retelling of the story involves all of the children. You will need someone to play the part of Moses, another to be Aaron, and a third to play Pharaoh. The rest of the children can play the parts of the Israelites. You will also need two large pieces of blue fabric to use as the Red Sea.

Last week we heard about the birth of Moses and how God kept him safe as he grew up. God had a very special job for Moses to do and he protected him from all sorts of things that happened to him. When he was an adult, God spoke to Moses and told him that he needed to speak to the Pharaoh to ask him to let his people go.

Bring Moses into the centre.

Moses was very scared about this, so God let his brother, Aaron, go too.

Bring Aaron to stand alongside Moses.

Moses and Aaron went to speak to the Pharaoh to tell him what God had said.

Aaron and Moses should stand before the Pharaoh and say, 'God says, let my people go.'

But Pharaoh refused. He wanted the slaves to stay in Egypt and carry on working hard for him. He wasn't about to let them go!

But no matter how powerful Pharaoh was, God was even more so and nothing could stop him from setting his people free. God sent ten horrible plagues, each one as a sign to the Pharaoh that he should listen to God.

As you list the plagues, counting them out on your fingers, Moses and Aaron should stand in front of the Pharaoh, while he continues to shake his head, with arms folded.

First, God turned the River Nile to blood *(1)*, then God sent frogs jumping all over *(2)*, gnats swarming across the land *(3)*, and flies filling the skies *(4)*.

Still Pharaoh refused to listen to God; he would not let the people go. Then the farm animals died: cows and camels, horses and goats *(5)*. There were sores, which hurt the Egyptians *(6)*, and hailstones fell hard from the sky *(7)*.

Pharaoh still would not let the people go. So God sent a plague of locusts to eat all the crops *(8)*, and darkness to fill the sky and black out the sun *(9)*.

But Pharaoh still would not let the Israelites go. Moses and Aaron warned Pharaoh that God was going to send the worst plague of all, but Pharaoh still said no. So God did as he had warned and the eldest son in every Egyptian family died *(10)*.

Now Pharaoh had had enough and ordered the Israelites to leave Egypt. At last God's people could go free!

Moses and Aaron led the people out of Egypt, but they had to stop when they reached the Red Sea.

All the children should move around until they reach the 'water', where they should stop.

Then God told Moses to hold his stick out across the water and, as he did so, God separated the water into two.

Two leaders should pull the two pieces of blue fabric back to divide the seas.

As the Israelites crossed through the water, the Egyptian army was chasing hard on their heels. Pharaoh had changed his mind.

Involve some leaders in playing the part of the Egyptian army.

But God would save his people again and when the Israelites reached the other side, God allowed the waters to flood back and completely cover the Egyptians.

Carefully cover the leaders with the blue fabric.

God had brought his people safely to the other side of the Red Sea and now they could begin their new life of freedom and safety.

Prayer

Father God, thank you for today's great big story, where you set your people free. Thank you that you love and care for us as your people too, and want to keep us safe from harm. Amen

Songs

Songs today could include:

- 'How did Moses cross the Red Sea' (Hugh Mitchell and J.C. Brumfield)
- 'No other God' (Paul Jones)

Take home

Suggest to the children that when they get home they can find out more about Moses and the Israelites, perhaps looking Moses up in a Bible or reading more stories about him in a children's Bible story book.

God's special rules

For the team

Refer to pages 6–8 to see how the activity areas work together

Session theme

During this final session of three exploring the life of Moses, we discover more about the way God gave the Israelites the ten commandments, his special rules, when Moses climbed Mount Sinai, and we think about what those rules mean to us, as followers of God, today.

Bible text: Exodus 19--20

Team prayer

Father God, you want the best for us, and set these rules for us to follow to show us the best way to live. Help us to share these rules with the children in a way that they can understand, and to share your heart of love for all people. Amen

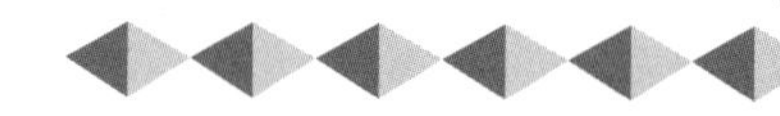

Activity areas

Small world play

Set up a desert scene in a sand tray, with a layer of sand, people and appropriate animal figurines and small tents (which can be made from small lengths of dowel and scraps of fabric). Invite the children to play through the way the Israelites wandered around in the desert once they had escaped from Egypt.

Talk about the way that the Israelites soon forgot how God had brought them to safety and started moaning and groaning. God had to give his people rules to remind them about the right way to live as his people.

Role play / dressing up

Set up a street scene with ride-on vehicles and dressing-up costumes for roles such as police officers and road crossing patrol officers. You could also provide some simple road signs such as Stop and Go. Encourage the children to role play how to use the road safely, following the instructions of those directing.

Talk about how some people have jobs which are specifically there to keep us safe. How do they tell us what to do and why should we do as they say?

Creative

Gather some cheap bars of soap and a selection of tools, such as old pencils and clay-marking tools. Invite the children to make engravings in the soap—perhaps a picture to go with the story, a few words or simply a pattern.

Talk about the way that God engraved his rules into the tablets of stone, to remind his people of what they were to do and of the agreement they had, to live in the right way, as people of God.

Construction

Provide modelling clay and invite the children to construct a model of a mountain which can be added to the small world play scene. You may find it helpful to provide some photographs of the mountain ranges in this area to help the children to create their models.

Talk about the way that God appeared to Moses on Mount Sinai and gave him the ten commandments, while the Israelites saw lightning on the mountain. This was a remarkable encounter for God's people, as described in the Bible.

Writing

Source a number of age-appropriate versions of the ten commandments and invite the children to work together as a group to write the ten commandments in their own words, in a way they can all understand.

Talk about the children's ideas for rewording the commandments. Explain any concepts they find difficult and encourage them to say what each of the commandments means to them.

Books

Display a selection of books with stories about Moses and his lifetime, alongside age-appropriate children's Bibles.

Share the books with the children, supporting them with reading as necessary. Talk about the way that God used all the things that happened to Moses in a positive way, taking him out of the negative situations that he found himself in, and moving him to a place of freedom and safety.

Games

Set up some well-known board games to play with the children, but ask a leader to play the games with the children, deliberately causing problems by breaking the rules and openly cheating.

Talk about what happens when we break the rules and why we have them in the first place. Why do you think God gave his people rules to follow?

Story time

Today's storytelling makes use of the ten rules that the children generated in the shared writing activity. It would be helpful to have each rule written out on a separate piece of card, for ten volunteers to hold up and read at the appropriate point. Ask the children to sit down with you.

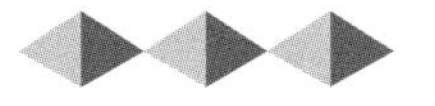

Do you remember in our last session we found out about how God set his people, the Israelites, free from slavery in Egypt? You would think, after everything they had been through, that they would enjoy their new lives, but actually it wasn't long before they were moaning and groaning again. God decided he had to do something for them. So God told Moses to do exactly what he said.

God came to the top of the mountain and told Moses to meet him there. The rest of the people had to stay down at the bottom of the mountain, because God is so holy and the people could not get close to him. When Moses got to the top of the mountain, God told him that the people needed to remember that he is their God and should live their lives in a way that made God happy. Then he gave Moses ten special rules, or commandments, for the people to follow.

Invite the ten volunteers to come up, one at a time, and read the rule on their card.

When God had finished speaking, he wrote the rules on two big stone slabs, to help the people to remember what he had said. Moses took the rules back down to the people to share what God had told them. Just like us today, people still did wrong things and broke the rules, but God loves all his people and wants to help us to learn to be a good follower of him.

Prayer

Father God, thank you for the rules that you gave us to keep us safe and show us the best way to live. Sometimes it can be hard to follow rules and we are sorry for the times when we get things wrong. Thank you that you forgive us and give us the chance to start again. Amen

Songs

Songs today could include:

- 'I can do all things' (Jim Bailey)

Take home

Provide copies of the ten commandments as worded in the writing activity during the session for the children to take home and display where they will be reminded of the things discussed during this session, and how we live life in the way that pleases God.

10
Joshua and the walls of Jericho

For the team

Refer to pages 6–8 to see how the activity areas work together

Session theme

This session explores the way that God enabled his people to enter Jericho in the most unlikely of ways, showing that nothing is too difficult for God, and he can do all things when we trust in him and the things that he says. Through this session, we will explore the story and how we, too, should show obedience to God.

Bible text: Joshua 6

Team prayer

Father God, thank you that nothing is too difficult for you. Help us to listen for your voice leading us in the decisions we make, and trusting as we follow you in every different circumstance. Amen

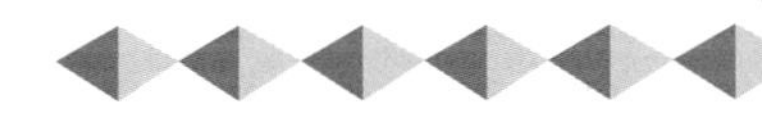

Activity areas

Small world play

A toy castle would work well for this session, along with appropriate play characters such as knights or soldiers. Encourage the children to think about the different roles that the characters play in defending the walls from attack.

Talk about the way that the walls of Jericho were a bit like a castle, but Joshua did not have to attack the walls in the usual way; he just had to follow God's instructions and God made it possible to destroy the walls of Jericho.

Role play / dressing up

Gather a selection of appropriate items of clothing for dressing up in armour. These could include breastplates, helmets, shields and knitted chainmail, among other things you can source, and could come in a variety of styles from different eras.

Talk about the different pieces of armour and how they were used at different times by those in battle.

Creative

Gather a selection of foil containers, silver foil and clean metallic packaging items, along with metallic coloured paint, scissors and glue, and invite the children to reuse the recycled items to make 'treasure' such as dishes and goblets.

Talk about God's instruction to his people to capture the gold and silver to put into the treasury, the place where special objects were kept for God. Why do you think these objects were kept for God?

Construction

Use building bricks to work together to build a model of what the city walls may have looked like.

Talk about how the city walls were built to protect the people in the city, but nothing can stop God and he was able to crush the walls easily.

Books

Provide a selection of children's Bibles and story books which retell the story of Joshua and the battle. You may find other books with illustrations of walled cities like Jericho.

Support the children in reading the books, where necessary, and discuss with them the things that interest them.

Prayer and reflective activity

Provide a number of party blowers and invite the children to blow them together, making as much noise as they can.

Talk about the way that the priests had to blow the horns when they had marched around, which caused the walls to fall. They followed God's instructions, no matter how strange or unlikely they sounded. How can we follow God's instructions too?

Games

A number of different tumbling themed games are appropriate for this age group, where children need to try to balance things and keep the whole structure from tumbling down (for example, Jenga). A selection of these games would work well in this session.

Story time

Today's retelling makes use of the scene created for the small world play activity (or use the walls created for the construction activity if you prefer) and gives the children an opportunity to participate by manipulating the play figures as you tell the story. Ask the children to sit in a circle around the model castle, and give each of them an appropriate play figure to represent Joshua, the priests and the army.

God's people had been wandering around in the wilderness for a very long time, still learning what it meant to be a follower of God and to do the things he told them to. This story takes place after Moses had died and a man called Joshua had been chosen by God to lead his people.

When the people approached the city of Jericho, God told Joshua that he would enable them to enter the city, but they would need to listen to God and do exactly as he said.

'First,' said God, 'the army and the priests need to march around the city walls, once each day, for six days.' So that is what they did.

Encourage the children to 'march' their play figures around the city six times.

'Then,' said God, 'on the seventh day, march around the walls seven times. When they march around for the seventh time, the priests must all blow their trumpets, and the army will shout!' So that is what they did.

Prompt the children to do so, with their play figures, adding the appropriate sound effects.

As they marched around for the final time, trumpets blasting and everyone shouting, the city walls all came tumbling down.

Encourage the children to knock the walls down.

And the people could enter the city, just as God had said.

Prayer

Father God, thank you that nothing is too big or too difficult for you. This story reminds us that if we trust in you, you will keep us safe and give us all that you promise. Amen

Songs

Songs today could include:

- 'Joshua and the battle of Jericho' (Anon)
- 'Quick on your feet again' (Ian Smale)

Take home

You could suggest that the children may wish to visit a castle or city walls, and to think about how impressive the walls of Jericho were, but nothing could stop God; he has power over all things.

11

Ruth: someone who cared

For the team

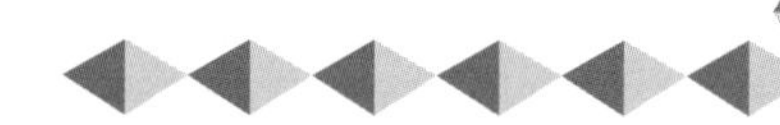

Refer to pages 6–8 to see how the activity areas work together

Session theme

This session celebrates the life of a humble hero who put the needs of her mother-in-law before her own. During this session, we consider how we can care for others, showing God's love for them and celebrating the fact that we are all members of God's great family.

Bible text: Ruth 1—4

Team prayer

Father God, thank you that you welcome us into your family, regardless of our status, position or background. Help us to extend that welcome and care to all those we meet, just as Ruth did for Naomi, and Boaz did for Ruth. Amen

Activity areas

Small world play

Set up a farm scene, perhaps using different grains to form a base, with fields, tractors, combine harvesters and hay bales, along with people figurines to act as farm workers. Encourage the children to act out the way that crops are gathered in.

Talk about how crops are harvested today, using large equipment. Explain that in the time of Ruth, farm workers would have gathered the crops by hand.

Role play / dressing up

Provide a selection of ride-on tractors and trailers as well as toy tools, including spades, rakes, watering cans, etc. Small sacks of grain or bundles of straw or hay would be a great addition to this area and children could also have access to wellington boots, overalls and jackets to play the role of farmers, taking care of the crops that they are growing.

Talk about Boaz the farmer, who cared for Ruth by giving her the opportunity to gather some food.

Creative

Present a selection of different grains, in a variety of sizes, colours and textures along with paper and PVA glue, and invite the children to create their own picture or pattern by collaging with the different grains. You could provide a simple line-drawn picture for the children to fill in each of the different sections, or allow children a free choice with the pictures that they wish to create.

Talk about the way that Ruth was allowed to gather grains left at the edge of the field when the workers were harvesting because she had no other food of her own.

Construction

Provide a number of seed trays and a selection of different grains and pulses, as well as appropriately coloured fun foam and fabric. Invite the children to create a farm scene in their seed tray using a selection of the materials provided. You could also provide small farm animals, or card for the children to construct and add extra details, such as barns, vehicles, and so on.

Talk about how we still get our food from farms today, but we just need to go to the supermarket to buy it. Ruth and Naomi understood where the food came from, because they were used to seeing it grow and harvesting it for themselves.

Writing

Provide a selection of thank-you cards, or craft materials which can be used by the children to make their own cards, along with pens and envelopes. Invite the children to write their own thank-you card to someone who cares for them, perhaps a family member or friend.

Talk about the way that Naomi was grateful to Ruth for taking care of her and wanted her to find happiness with Boaz. Do we show gratitude to the people who care for us?

Books

Along with the children's Bible story books and retellings of the story of Ruth, you could provide a selection of books on the theme of family.

Support the children in reading the books, where necessary, and discuss with them the things that interest them.

Prayer and reflective activity

Provide a large sheet of paper and pens. Invite the children to draw pictures, or write the names of the different people who care for them, or people that they care for. Encourage the children to pray as they do so, to thank God for these people and the role that they play in our lives.

Talk about the way that Ruth cared for Naomi, Naomi cared for Ruth, and Boaz cared for Ruth and her family. God gave us people to care for us and who we can care for too.

Story time

For this retelling of the story, you will need three volunteers (children or adult helpers) who can mime the roles of Naomi, Ruth and Boaz appropriately as you tell the story. You could also invite volunteers to stand at the beginning of the story, to represent Orpah, Elimelech, Mahlon and Chilion.

This is the story of a family and how they took care of one another. There once was a lady named Naomi who had a husband and two sons, who were both grown up and married.

Sadly, Naomi's husband and sons all died, leaving Naomi, Ruth and Orpah. There was no food in the land where they lived, so Naomi decided to travel back to her homeland. She told Ruth and Orpah that they should go back home to their own families and start a new life with them.

But Ruth cared very much for Naomi, so she decided to travel with her.

Naomi and Ruth can walk together around the space.

When they reached Naomi's homeland, Ruth went out to find somewhere she could find food and met Boaz. She explained that she had travelled with Naomi and wanted to work to be able to look after her.

Ruth and Boaz should mime their conversation, as you continue.

Boaz owned some land. He knew Naomi and was very impressed that Ruth wanted to care for her, so he invited Ruth to gather the crops that she needed to eat from his own fields.

Ruth should mime gathering the crops to give to Naomi.

After a while, Boaz decided he wanted to take greater care of Ruth, so they got married!

So Ruth had cared for Naomi, and Boaz cared for them both. God brought this family together and they cared for each other.

Prayer

Father God, thank you for our families, who love and care for us. Help us to care for our own families, and for other people who may need our help. Amen

Songs

Songs today could include:

- 'Big family of God' (Becky Drake)

Take home

Suggest the children talk to their families about finding opportunities to welcome other people into their family lives, perhaps hosting a special meal for someone who does not have a lot of family around them.

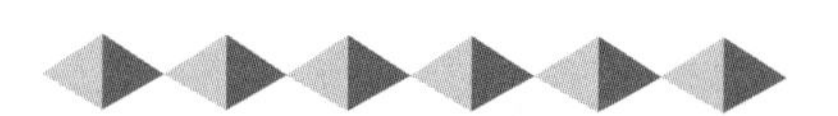

12

Samuel: a boy who listened

For the team

Refer to pages 6–8 to see how the activity areas work together

Session theme

Through this session, we discover the way that God chose to speak to Samuel, a young boy, reminding us that God doesn't just work through those of great position and status. During this session, we will explore the ways that we can listen to hear God speak to us, just as he spoke to Samuel.

Bible text: 1 Samuel 3

Team prayer

Father God, thank you that when we speak to you, you hear our prayers and will always answer. Help us to listen for your voice, speaking to us, and to do the things that you say. Amen

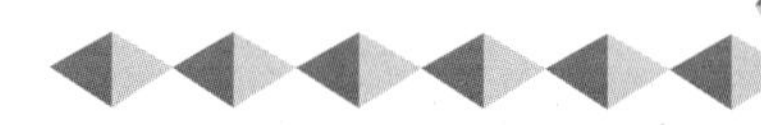

Activity areas

Small world play

Provide a doll's house which includes both a child's bedroom and an adult's bedroom along with a number of people figures. Encourage the children to think about the things that they do at bedtime, and the other things they may do in their own bedroom.

Talk about the way that God spoke to Samuel when he was in bed. Samuel woke Eli up, thinking it was him calling, but Eli helped him to understand that it was God.

Role play / dressing up

Provide some old telephone or mobile phone handsets, along with notebooks or clipboards, paper and pens. Invite the children to role play working in an office, using the telephones to make or receive phone calls, and taking messages to pass on.

Talk about how you need to listen carefully when you are taking a message for someone else, just as Samuel did when listening to God.

Creative

Provide a number of plain headbands, along with card or felt, scissors, pens and staplers. Make different distinctive ear shapes (rabbit, elephant, cat, and so on) from the card or felt before fastening them to the headbands for children to wear.

Talk about how we use our ears to listen to different sounds. God speaks to us in different ways and it's not always a voice that we can hear out loud.

Writing

Display a large piece of paper on the wall and invite the children to add their own 'questions to ask God'.

Talk about the way that God spoke to Samuel, even though he was only a young boy. The questions that we have matter to God, he wants to help us to learn more about him. Talk about the different questions that children add.

Books

Books offered today could include a selection of children's Bibles and story books which tell this and other stories of Samuel.

Support the children in reading the books, where necessary, and discuss with them the things that interest them.

Prayer and reflective activity

Set up a quiet zone, perhaps using a gazebo or similar structure as a way of denoting this area as separate from the noisier activities. You could also use soft cushions, battery-operated candles or coloured lights, Bible story books, a cross, other helpful images and paper and pens.

Talk about how this area can be used and encourage the children to remain quiet in it. It may be helpful to sit with the children, perhaps only for short periods of time, and talk later about the issues that are raised, as appropriate.

Games

This would be a good session to play some listening games, such as Chinese Whispers or the Shopping List game, where the children have to listen carefully and remember the things that have been mentioned before. There is also a parachute game that children could play, where, while everyone holds on to the edge of the parachute, a leader calls out, 'Run under if... [for example, you have blonde hair, are wearing trainers, and so on].' If the end of the sentence is relevant to them, the children have to run under the parachute and swap places with another player, while the rest of the group holds the parachute up in the air.

Story time

This story will need two volunteers to play the parts of Samuel and Eli, perhaps one child and one leader. Provide a blanket for each of them to use, as they lie on their beds.

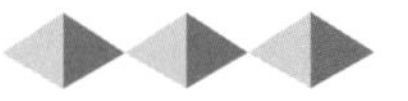

There once was a boy called Samuel who lived in the temple with Eli the priest.

One night, as they lay down to sleep, Samuel heard a voice calling his name: 'Samuel, Samuel.' Samuel thought that Eli must be calling him, so he got out of bed and went to see Eli.

Samuel should go to Eli and say, 'Here I am. What do you want?'

Eli was very surprised to see Samuel. He had been fast asleep! So he sent Samuel back to bed. When Samuel was lying down once again, he heard someone calling his name: 'Samuel, Samuel.'

So again, Samuel got out of bed and went to see Eli.

Samuel should go to Eli again and say, 'Here I am. What do you want?'

But Eli was surprised to see Samuel again. He hadn't called Samuel, so he sent him back to bed. Samuel settled down to sleep again, but it wasn't long before someone called his name again: 'Samuel, Samuel.'

Samuel got out of bed again, and went to see Eli.

For a third time, Samuel should go to Eli and say, 'Here I am. What do you want?'

Eli woke up yet again, surprised to see Samuel. He hadn't called him. Then he realised what must have been happening. It wasn't Eli who had been calling Samuel, it was God! So Eli told Samuel to go back to bed and to listen. He told Samuel that if he heard God calling his name again, he should say, 'I'm listening, God. What do you want me to do?'

So that's exactly what Samuel did. He went back to bed, and when he heard someone calling his name again, he said, 'I'm listening, God. What do you want me to do?'

Samuel listened as God spoke to him, giving him a special message to share with Eli. This was the first time that Samuel heard God speak to him, but it wouldn't be the last. God often gave messages to Samuel to share with people, and Samuel listened to the things that God said.

Prayer

Dear God, thank you that we can speak to you about the things that matter to us, and you always listen. Thank you that you can speak to us too. Help us to listen to you and to learn to hear your voice, just as Samuel did. Amen

Songs

Songs today could include:

- 'When you are sleeping' (Becky Drake)
- 'Your eyes' (David Wakerly, Beci Wakerly and Julia A'Bell)

Take home

Talk to the children about how they can pray when they are at home. Encourage them to take time to be quiet, when they are praying, to let God speak to them. Make space to continue to talk to the children about this in the coming weeks.

13

David and Goliath

For the team

Refer to pages 6–8 to see how the activity areas work together

Session theme

This is the first in a series of three sessions about David, during which we explore the well-known story of the young man who slew the mighty giant, using only a slingshot and a pebble. Through this session, we will think about what it means to have total confidence that God is unfailing and can do all things, just as David trusted when he stood in front of Goliath.

Bible text: 1 Samuel 17

Team prayer

Father God, thank you that nothing is too difficult for you and you can do all things. Help us to really grasp what this means for us today, and to share this story with the children with whom we work. Amen

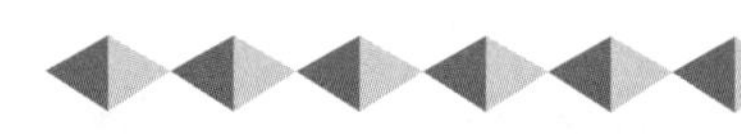

Activity areas

Small world play

Set up a scene where the children can retell this story, with play figures to represent the two armies facing each other, and a much larger play figure to represent Goliath. You could also include the land where David cared for his sheep, and a river where he gathered the pebbles.

Talk to the children about the story as they retell it with the play figures. Help them to remember the important details to include, as they do so.

Role play / dressing up

Provide a selection of items of adult-sized clothing, which will be too big for the children to wear, and encourage them to try some of these clothes on.

Talk about how silly they felt when they tried on clothes that were all too big for them. Saul wanted David to wear his armour to protect him when he fought Goliath but it was all far too big. Can God only use us when we are big enough?

Creative

Set out a large sheet of paper and draw a life-size outline of Goliath. Provide paints and paintbrushes and invite the children to work together to complete the painting, adding the appropriate features and details.

Talk about the children's impressions of Goliath as they include them in the painting, thinking about his scary appearance and expression.

Construction

Gather a supply of cardboard boxes and challenge the children to work together to build a tower as high as they can, before the tower topples. This could be organised as a group challenge, where all the children work together, or as a competition with opposing teams.

Talk about how tall Goliath was in relation to the towers that they build. Our towers topple easily, but can you imagine trying to knock down a giant?

Writing

Set out a large roll of paper and provide pens in a selection of sizes, including large, thick marker pens. Invite the children to experiment with writing in a range of styles and sizes, both large and small.

Talk about our experiences of large and small, and how David, the smallest person in this story, defeated Goliath, the largest.

Books

Books offered today should include children's Bibles and books about this event and others from David's lifetime. You could also offer a selection of books about sheep and shepherding, as well as fictitious stories about giants.

Support the children in reading the books, where necessary, and discuss with them the things that interest them.

Prayer and reflective activity

Set out a selection of small pebbles and invite the children to hold one each, as you pray together.

Talk about how David, who was only small, used one little pebble to defeat Goliath. Do you think David felt small? When do we feel small? God used David to defeat Goliath because he trusted God to help him. How can we trust God to help us too?

Story time

Today's story takes place around the small world play area, where children can manipulate the play figures at the appropriate points in the story. Invite the children to sit around the scenery with you.

God's people were in trouble. They were facing an enemy, a great and powerful army with one key weapon, a giant warrior called Goliath. Every day, Goliath would come out and face God's people.

'Who dares to fight me?' called Goliath.

And every day, God's people would run away and hide.

One day, a young boy called David was sent to find his brothers at the battleground and take them food from home. When he got to the front line, he heard Goliath calling, 'Who dares to fight me?'

David was shocked to see God's people running away. He couldn't believe that nobody would stand up to fight Goliath.

'We are God's people!' he said. 'God will help us to defeat this man.'

Everybody was very surprised when David came forward to fight against the giant. He was so small, and Goliath was so big! But David trusted God to help him. He gathered together five small stones from the river, putting the first one into his sling. Then he spun the sling around his head, and whoosh! The stone flew through the air and hit Goliath on the head, knocking him to the ground and killing him with one blow!

God's people had become scared when they saw Goliath, but David remembered that no matter how small we may feel, God is bigger than any enemy we may face.

Prayer

Father God, thank you that no matter how small we feel, you are always with us and through you, we can do all things, just like David. Amen

Songs

Songs today could include:

- 'Nothing's too big' (Doug Horley)
- 'Our God is a great big God' (Nigel and Jo Hemming)

Take home

Challenge the children to look out for really small things and really tall things this week, as a reminder of today's story and how God can work through us, even when we feel very small.

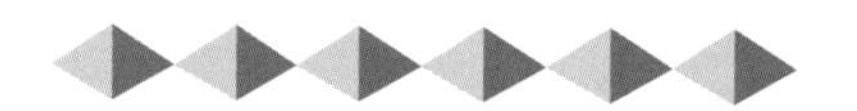

14 David and Jonathan

For the team

Refer to pages 6–8 to see how the activity areas work together

Session theme

This is the second in a series of three, exploring events from the life of David. During this session we will discover more about his friendship with Jonathan, the son of the king who wanted him dead, and the way that the young prince supported and protected his friend, even when that meant putting himself in danger.

Bible text: 1 Samuel 18—20

Team prayer

Father God, thank you that you bring people into our lives to walk alongside us, in the good times and when times are difficult. Help us to model friendship, as Jonathan did, looking out for others and putting their needs first. Amen

Activity areas

Small world play

Set up a countryside scene, with a range of terrains, using large stones to represent mountains and incorporating caves. You could also include sheep in the scene to remind the children of David's old life. Use play figures to represent David and Jonathan, Saul and his army and encourage the children to retell the story of David's escape from Saul.

Talk about how David's life was quite an adventure—from being a shepherd boy to living in the royal family—and how he found himself running away from a king who wanted to kill him. How must he have felt?

Role play / dressing up

Gather a selection of 'royalty' themed dressing-up outfits, such as cloaks and crowns, princess dresses and tiaras. You could also set up a large chair which the children can decorate, perhaps by draping over appropriate fabrics or hanging tinsel over it, to create a throne.

Talk about David's move to the palace of Saul and his family. Living with the royal family would have been a very different experience for David, who had grown up taking care of the sheep!

Creative

Provide strips of gold or silver card along with sparkly sequins, gems and other appropriate collage materials, scissors and glue. Invite the children to make and decorate their own shiny crown, assisting with measuring and securing around their heads once complete.

Talk about the way that Saul stopped listening to God and became a bad king. What makes a good leader or a bad leader of the people?

Construction

Provide small building bricks and bases, along with the appropriate play figures, and invite the children to design and build their own royal palace, thinking about all the different rooms that they may include. You could also provide images of well-known royal palaces or castles as a stimulus for this activity.

Talk about how Saul would not have lived in a palace as we are used to seeing, but it still would have been a special place for the royal family.

Writing

Provide some blank postcards, together with felt pens and pencils. Invite the children to decorate a postcard, before writing a message on the other side, ready to send or give the card to a friend. This should be a message of thanks or encouragement to somebody they care about.

Talk about what makes our friends special to us and the children's ideas about what they want to write in a message to their friends, as they do so.

Books

Alongside children's Bibles and books about David and his life, you could also provide a selection of stories with friendship as a theme.

Support the children in reading the books, where necessary, and discuss with them the things that interest them.

Prayer and reflective activity

Provide small strips of paper and work together with the children to concertina-fold the paper into four segments. Draw a simple person outline on the front segment and show the children how to cut it out so that they have a paper chain of four connected people. Provide pens and pencils for the children to decorate the people, before writing their own name on one and the name of three of their friends on the other three segments.

Talk about the children's friends and why they are special to them. What can we thank God for, when we think about these friends? What can we ask God for?

Games

Games played today could include hide and seek or treasure hunting games. You could also invite the children to share some of their favourite games that they play with their own friends.

Story time

Ask two of your leaders to play the parts of David and Jonathan and to learn the script below, or ad lib appropriately if they prefer.

Do you remember last week when we found out more about David who defeated the giant, Goliath? After that, he went to live with Saul, the king. His best friend was Jonathan, Saul's son. Together, they were great friends, who took care of one another. Today, we are going to find out more about their friendship and the things that they got up to together.

Introduce the two leaders playing the roles of David and Jonathan.

David: Hello everybody, my name is David, you might remember me from another story. I fought against Goliath and, with God's help, I killed the giant. Then I went to live with King Saul, in his royal palace. I often played my harp to help calm the king. I also met Saul's son, Jonathan. We are very good friends.

Jonathan: I was really glad when David came to live at the palace. It was good to have someone to spend time with, and David did a great job keeping Dad calm. He does get very cross sometimes.

David: Sometimes, Saul's actions worried the crowds. They didn't know what to do. Most of the time, they would call for me, and I would play my harp for him. But one day, things changed. I couldn't calm Saul down, no matter what I did. Saul wanted to kill me!

Jonathan: So I helped David to escape, far away from the palace, into the hillside nearby, where he hid in a cave.

David: It wasn't the only time Saul would come looking to hurt me. There would be many more times when I would need to run away. It was another opportunity to trust God to take care of me, against the enemy.

Jonathan: But David never hurt my dad. He didn't want to fight with him; he always thought about what God would want him to do.

David: And God continued to keep me safe.

Prayer

Father God, thank you for our friends. Help us to be a good friend to others, caring for them and acting in a way that makes you happy. Amen

Songs

Songs today could include:

- 'Never give up' (Brittany Grey)
- 'Wonderful Lord' (Doug Horley)

Take home

Invite the children to take their postcards away with them to give to their friends this week.

15

King David praises God

For the team

Refer to pages 6–8 to see how the activity areas work together

Session theme

This is the final session in a series of three, looking at events from the life of David. This session explores the way that David worshipped God through song, music and dancing and how he began the process of building the temple, which his son would later complete.

Bible text: 1 Chronicles 17 and 22—29

Team prayer

Almighty God, thank you for who you are and what you do. May our lives and our service to you demonstrate what it means for us to be able to worship you, as your children. Amen

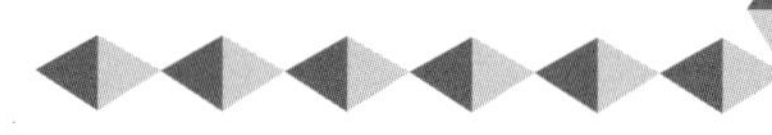

Activity areas

Small world play

Set up a town scene, perhaps using some simple houses made from cardboard boxes and a number of people figurines and in different places around the scene, hide some of the items that would have been used to build the temple, such as rocks, small pieces of wood and 'precious gems'. Encourage the children to re-enact what happened when David called for these items to be gathered together (see 1 Chronicles 22).

Talk about the way that David involved the people in gathering the things together. The temple would be a very special place for God's people and they wanted to help David.

Role play / dressing up

Provide clipboards and pens with a checklist of items that children need to find from around the room. The checklist could be provided in word form and in pictures to include all children in this activity. Invite the children to search for the objects, ticking them off as they find them.

Talk about how David had a list of materials he wanted the people to gather together to be used to build the temple.

Creative

Collect a number of items of clean junk modelling materials, such as plastic bottles, yogurt pots, cardboard boxes, and other useful items such as elastic bands, string, paper, sticky tape and grains. Invite the children to design and make their own recycled instrument, such as shakers, 'harps' whose strings can be plucked and small drums. They can then decorate their completed instrument, perhaps with coloured papers, stickers or paint.

Talk about the different instruments that they have created and how they can play them. David played the harp and wrote songs or psalms which he used to worship God.

Construction

Provide small building bricks and invite the children to design and build their own temple or special building for God. You may wish to provide pictures of the temple as well as some of our historic cathedral buildings.

Talk about the way that David began to gather the materials together for the temple, but it was his son who completed the work. God no longer lives in a building, but we can still use our creativity to show God how much we love him.

Writing

Put up a large sheet of paper and write the heading, 'God, you are…'. Invite the children to add their own words and phrases to the sheet using different coloured pens.

Talk about the children's own ideas as they add them to the sheet, and why they have chosen to include those words. Encourage the children to feel free in the words that they choose to use.

Books

Provide a selection of children's Bibles and books about the life of David, as well as children's books of psalms, poems and prayers.

Read and share the stories with the children as appropriate, supporting their reading as necessary. Explain that David wrote many of the psalms in the Bible which we still use in our prayers and singing today.

Prayer and reflective activity

Display a large copy of Psalm 23 and explain that David related what he understood about God to the things that were familiar to him, for example, shepherding. Put up the first few words of each line, and invite the children to work together with you to complete each line of the psalm with things that are familiar to them: The Lord's my…

Talk about the children's different ideas and why they want to include them. How does this help us to celebrate our relationship with God?

Story time

Today's story provides an opportunity to think more about the character and person of David, particularly the way he worshipped God. Before you begin, set out a large piece of paper and sketch out an outline drawing of David that the children can help to paint, as you continue to talk.

Over the last two weeks, we've been thinking about David and the way he trusted God in the different circumstances in which he found himself. There were times when David made mistakes and did things wrong but he praised God with his whole life, using the gifts and skills that God had given him. Sometime after Saul had died, David became the new king, just as God had promised David when he was very young.

David wrote and performed some beautiful songs, or psalms, many of which we can read in our Bibles today. He was a musician too, playing the harp as he sang his songs. David also often danced, as though he were putting on a concert to an audience of one, to God.

There was one more thing that David wanted to do, to show how important God was in his life. He wanted to build the most beautiful temple, filled with the most precious things to be used by the priests as they did God's works. He drew up the plans, and sent out men to gather together the different materials that they would need: wood and stones, iron and bronze, silver, gold and precious jewels.

All the things they would need were safely gathered together, ready to build the temple. It would be many more years before David's son, Solomon, would build the temple, but eventually the work would be complete and a place was created where everyone could praise God, just as David did.

Prayer

Father God, you are amazing, incredible and awesome. Thank you that we can praise you with singing and dancing, painting and writing. Amen

Songs

Songs today could include:

- 'He is the one' (Andrew and Pauline Pearson)
- 'I can't run enough' (Dave Godfrey)

Take home

Encourage the children to find ways of praising God in their own homes, this week. This could include singing songs, creating their own 'God, you are...' poster, dancing to praise music, and so on.

16

Elijah and the fire

For the team

Refer to pages 6–8 to see how the activity areas work together

Session theme

This session retells one story from the life of Elijah, the prophet, when God demonstrated his power and authority by sending fire down on the altar, in front of King Ahab and the prophets of Baal. During this session, we will remind the children that nothing is too difficult for God.

Bible text: 1 Kings 18

Team prayer

Almighty God, thank you that you have power and authority over all things. Help us to grasp hold of the truth that whatever we are dealing with, nothing is too difficult for you, and to share this truth with the children we work with. Amen

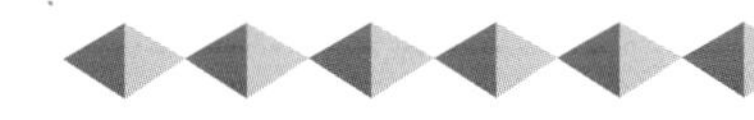

Activity areas

Small world play

Provide building blocks for the children to use to build an altar, and playdough in red, orange and yellow for the children to use to create flames which they can stick to one of the altars, as they re-enact what happened in the story.

Talk about what happened in the story. Can the children imagine what it would have been like to be there that day?

Role play / dressing up

Set up a post office area with paper, pens, envelopes and stamps for printing. Invite the children to write and post letters before delivering them, perhaps to other children in the room.

Talk about the way that we send and receive messages in the post. Talk about how Elijah brought his messages from God.

Creative

Provide sheets of paper and paint in a variety of 'fire' colours, along with plastic forks and combs. Create fire paintings by pouring a small amount of each of the fire colours in the centre of the paper and spread the paint out in all directions with the combs or forks.

Talk about the way that God sent fire down on to the altar. There is nothing that God cannot do.

Construction

Gather twelve equally sized stones and invite the children to try to build an altar, just as they did in the story. Challenge the children to see how many different ways they can organise the stones to build their model altars.

Talk about the way that people had to build altars, in the times of Elijah, to make a sacrifice to God, but because Jesus went to the cross, we don't need to any more!

Writing

Provide a selection of postcards and pens and invite the children to write a message to a friend or family member, which they can take away with them at the end of the session.

Talk about how Elijah was a messenger from God, who reminded people to listen to them. How can we tell our friends about God?

Books

Books offered today could include children's story Bibles and books which retell this story, as well as other stories about Elijah.

Support the children in reading the books, where necessary, and discuss with them the things that interest them.

Prayer and reflective activity

Provide some crown templates (see page 124) and a selection of craft materials which the children can use to decorate their crowns, including shiny papers, sticky gems, and so on. Invite the children to decorate a crown to wear, and to think about what it means for God to be the king in our own lives.

Talk about the way that Ahab was a bad king, because he did not honour God. God can be king of our lives if we listen to the things that he says and try to do them.

Story time

This story is told through the use of fabric visual aids, built up layer by layer, as you tell the story. For smaller groups, this could be done on a fabric base on the floor with the children seated around. For larger groups you may wish to prepare a board or banner which can be hung in front of the children.

Set out a large neutral-coloured piece of fabric as a base.

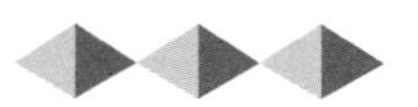

Elijah was a prophet, a messenger of God. He had to give people messages from God, telling them when they needed to change their ways and listen to God again.

One day, God sent Elijah to speak to King Ahab, to warn him that there would be no rain until Ahab stopped worshipping Baal and started worshipping the real God. Then he showed King Ahab exactly what God could do.

He called together the prophets who followed Baal and King Ahab, and took them all up Mount Carmel. Then he told Baal's prophets to build an altar, so they did, stone by stone.

Lay out some small, grey felt rock shapes to build an altar.

Then he asked them to choose their offering to lay on the altar.

Lay a red piece of felt on top of the altar.

He challenged the prophets to pray to Baal to ask him to send fire. So they danced and sang, they shouted and prayed. But nothing happened at all.

'Perhaps your god has gone to sleep,' laughed Elijah. 'Or maybe he's gone to the toilet!'

Then Elijah built his altar to God.

Lay out twelve small, grey felt rock shapes to build an altar alongside the first.

He dug a trench all around the altar.

Lay a narrow strip of black felt around the base of the altar.

He placed his offering on the altar.

Place a red piece of felt at the top of the altar.

Before pouring water all over it.

Use small pieces of blue felt to represent the water, sprinkled over the offering and filling the trench below.

Then Elijah prayed. And as he did, God sent fire which burned the offering and the altar!

Use red, orange and yellow flame shapes to cover the altar.

Everyone could then see that God is the true God. They all worshipped him. And then God sent the rain once again.

Prayer

Dear God, thank you that you listen to our prayers, just as you listened to Elijah. You are the true God and nothing is too difficult for you! Amen.

Songs

Songs today could include:

- 'No other God' (Paul Jones)

Take home

Encourage the children to take some time this week to think about how we can make sure we treat God as a king in our own lives, and don't put others above him.

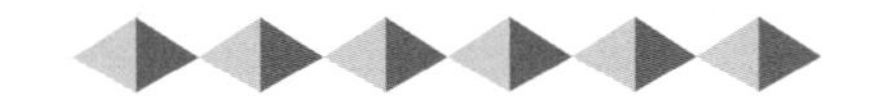

17

Daniel and the lions

For the team

Refer to pages 6–8 to see how the activity areas work together

Session theme

During this session, we will explore this well-known story, giving thanks for the courage with which Daniel acted, choosing to pray to God even when he knew the risks that he was taking. We will also remember that God is always with us, protecting us, just as he protected Daniel.

Bible text: Daniel 6

Team prayer

Father God, thank you for the example that Daniel set, trusting you even when it came at a great cost. We may not find ourselves in such danger, but we know that you are always with us too, and will protect us from harm. Amen

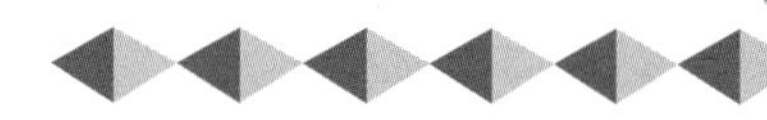

Activity areas

Small world play

Set up a scene which children can use to retell the story. You could include play figures to represent Daniel, Darius and the three administrators, lions and an angel.

Talk about the story as the children retell it, helping them to remember the key events and details.

Role play / dressing up

Provide a selection of appropriate costumes for the children to use to retell the story. These could include lion masks, angel dressing-up costumes, a crown and royal robes. You could also set up a special chair as a throne and a playpen to use as the den.

Talk about how the children feel about each of the characters and what they did in the story. Why do they think the different characters chose to act in the way that they did?

Creative

Prepare a large outline of an angel, drawn on to a large sheet of paper, and provide a selection of appropriate collage materials including papers, fabrics, sequins, and so on. Invite the children to help you to complete the collaged angel, selecting materials and covering the outlined image.

Talk about the way that God sent the angel to close the mouths of the lions and keep Daniel safe. We know very little about what angels really look like; talk about the children's own ideas as they help with the collaging.

Construction

Gather a supply of large cardboard boxes, along with wide sticky tape and scissors. Work together with the children to construct a den, where the lions were kept, along with a large stone which could be used to seal the den closed.

Talk about how scary it would be to find yourself in a den full of lions! Daniel must have been very frightened, but God kept him safe.

Books

Books offered today could include children's story Bibles and story books about Daniel. You may also find age-appropriate information about the persecuted Church, to share with the children.

Support the children in reading the books, where necessary, and discuss with them the things that interest them.

Prayer and reflective activity

Provide post-it notes and pens and invite the children to stick their prayers on to a window.

Talk about the way that Daniel stood at the window to pray to God, even though he knew he was breaking the king's new rules because he wouldn't stop worshipping God.

Games

Games played today could include the traditional game Sleeping Lions, where the children should lie completely still, trying not to move. Anyone caught moving is out.

Story time

Today's story time makes use of the materials used in the small world play activity, involving the children in manipulating the figures as you tell the story. Seat the children around the scene and explain to them how you would like them to play out the story, as you read the script below.

There once was a man called Daniel who was a follower of God. He and his friends had been moved a long way from home to a country where Darius was king.

Darius liked Daniel and promoted him to an important job. But the other people who worked for Darius were jealous of Daniel's new position and tricked Darius into creating rules which would make it difficult for God's people to follow God. The most awful thing that they did was to create a law that everyone in the land had to pray to Darius alone!

Daniel knew that he would be breaking the law if he prayed to God. But he also knew that God's rules were more important, and no matter what Darius did to punish him, he must put God first. So, very bravely, Daniel continued to stand at his window, where he could be seen by everyone, and pray to Father God.

Of course, one day as he was doing this, Darius' helpers spotted Daniel and brought him to the king for breaking the rules. Even though it made him very sad, Darius had to follow the rules he had set and Daniel had to be punished by being thrown into a den full of lions!

All that night Darius worried about what would happen to Daniel, and first thing in the morning, he rushed to the lions' den to see what had happened to him.

Darius was shocked to discover that Daniel was absolutely unharmed, without a scratch on him! The lions had barely even sniffed Daniel, let alone touched him. When Darius called Daniel out of the lions' den, Daniel explained that God had sent an angel who had closed the mouths of the lions, keeping him safe and sound.

Darius was so relieved. He changed the law he had made and told his people that from that day onwards, everyone should follow Daniel's God, and pray only to him.

Prayer

Father God, thank you for people like Daniel who show us how we should put you first, when it is easy and when it is difficult. Thank you that you protected Daniel and you will be with us too, when we choose to worship you. Amen

Songs

Songs today could include:

- 'All through history' (Becky Drake)
- 'No other God' (Paul Jones)

Take home

Encourage the children to spend some time this week praying for those people who, like Daniel, do not have the opportunity to pray openly to God, that he would protect them and keep them safe.

18

Jonah: God's messenger

For the team

Refer to pages 6–8 to see how the activity areas work together

Session theme

During this session, we discover more about the story of Jonah, the reluctant prophet. God demonstrated his heart of forgiveness to Jonah and how he would give a second chance, both to Jonah and to the people of Nineveh.

Bible text: Jonah 1—4

Team prayer

Father God, thank you that no matter what we do or where we go, you always welcome us back and give us the chance to start again. Help us to share this heart of forgiveness and fresh starts with the children we work with today. Amen

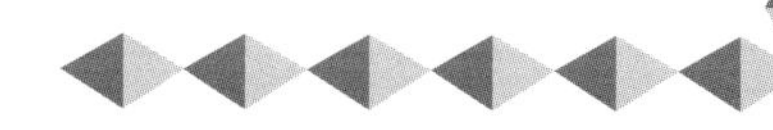

Activity areas

Small world play

Set up a scene which the children can use to retell the story. This would work well in a large water tray, where you can create different areas of land around the edge. Provide play figures to represent Jonah and other characters in the story, as well as a boat and large fish, or whale.

Talk to the children about what happened in the story, as they retell each part and act it out. Why do they think Jonah acted in the way that he did? How would he have felt at each stage of the story?

Role play / dressing up

Set up an office or post office scene, with telephones, paper and envelopes, postcards, clipboards, and so on. Invite the children to role play working in that setting, taking messages and passing them on, or delivering them to people elsewhere in the room.

Talk about the way that Jonah had a message from God, but rather than delivering the message as asked, he chose to run and hide.

Creative

Gather a number of rubber gloves and cut the fingers off. Provide a number of permanent marker pens, in a range of colours, which can be used under supervision to decorate a rubber glove finger and create a worm finger puppet.

Talk about the way that Jonah sat under the fig tree, at the end of the story, and became upset when the worm ate it up. God used this to show Jonah how he loved the people in Nineveh, and loved Jonah too.

Construction

Gather some large cardboard boxes and work together as a group to build a large model boat, perhaps adding a mast and sail. Can you fit your whole group in the boat?

Talk about the way that Jonah tried to get away from God by travelling in a boat. No matter where we go, God is always there.

Writing

Provide a number of resources that can be used for writing, which enable the writer to easily wipe away what they have done before starting again, such as dry wipe boards and pens, chalkboards and chalks and magnetic drawing toys.

Talk about how easy it is to clear your mistakes, when using one of these and starting again. God wants to give us the chance to start again, too, whenever we do something wrong.

Books

Books offered today could include children's Bibles and story books retelling the story of Jonah. You could also provide a selection of books about boats and fish, and atlases to point out the places on a map where this story took place.

Support the children in reading the books, where necessary, and discuss with them the things that interest them.

Prayer and reflective activity

Lay out a map of your local area, and highlight key points of interest for the children, such as the place where they meet, their schools, and so on.

Talk about Jonah and how God wanted him to travel to a particular place to tell the people there that he loved them, and they needed to change their ways. Where are the places that God wants us to go to tell people about him?

Games

Games you play today could include North, South, East, West, thinking about the time Jonah spent on a boat, and how he tried to travel in the opposite direction to where God had told him to go.

Story time

This story retelling makes use of the scene created for the children to use in the small world play activity. Depending upon the children's prior knowledge of the story, they may be able to retell parts of the story themselves. Set up the scene as described in the activity detailed above in the centre of the room and invite the children to sit around the edge so that everyone can see.

Hold up the figure representing Jonah.

This is the story of a man called Jonah. God gave him an important message to take to the people in a city called Nineveh, but Jonah didn't want to do this job. He thought God was being too kind to the people. Let's see what happened.

Stand Jonah on the central bank of land.

One day, Jonah heard God calling him. He told Jonah to go to the town of Nineveh, to tell the people there that God loved them, and that they were behaving in a way that upset God. They needed to change their ways.

But Jonah didn't want to go to Nineveh. He thought he could run away and hide from God, so he found a boat that was heading in the opposite direction, and paid the captain to take him with them.

Stand Jonah in the boat with other figures, and begin to 'sail' the boat towards one bank of land.

Jonah could not escape from God. He knew exactly where Jonah was and what he was up to, but God wanted to give Jonah another chance to do the right thing. So God sent a great big storm.

Encourage the children to make appropriate sound effects, and rock the boat.

Jonah knew that it was God who had sent the storm, and he knew what he had to do, so he told the ship's crew to throw him overboard. They didn't really want to, but Jonah convinced them it was the right thing to do, so they threw him out of the boat and into the deep, deep ocean.

You might think that Jonah was in danger, but God kept him safe. He sent along an enormous fish who swallowed Jonah whole.

Act out Jonah being thrown from the boat, as a fish comes along to swallow him up.

Jonah stayed in the fish's smelly belly for three whole days. He had no idea where he was. He was very scared. He prayed to God and said, 'I know I did the wrong thing, but you can rescue me. If you give me the chance, I will make this right and do what you asked me to do.'

So God sent the fish, with Jonah inside, to a sandy beach...

Move the fish to the third bank of land.

... where the fish spat Jonah out.

Position the Jonah figure on the bank of land.

And now Jonah did what God had told him. He gave the people of Nineveh God's warning to change their ways, and they all listened to what he had to say and told God that they were sorry. God forgave the people and gave them another chance, just as he had for Jonah.

Now, you might think that this would make Jonah happy—after all, it's what God had done for him—but it didn't. Jonah was cross with God for forgiving the people; he wanted God to be angry with them, and to punish them for doing wrong things. But God gently reminded Jonah that he had given him a second chance when he tried to run away from God, and now he was doing the same for the Ninevites, because he loves us all the same.

Prayer

Thank you, God, that you give second chances whenever we say sorry to you. Please help us to listen to the things you say to us, and to do the things that you say. Amen

Songs

Songs today could include:

- 'I can do all things' (Jim Bailey)
- 'If I've been wrong' (Sammy Horner)

Take home

Challenge the children to look for an opportunity this week to tell one of their friends that God loves them, just as Jonah told the people of Nineveh.

New Testament stories

19

Mary and the angel

For the team

Refer to pages 6–8 to see how the activity areas work together

Session theme

This is the first session to explore the stories of the New Testament, and looks at the way that Mary discovered she would give birth to Jesus. Through this session, we will explore her obedience to God and willingness to play her part in God's big story.

Bible text: Luke 1:26–38

Team prayer

Father God, thank you for Mary's obedience to you, and the example that she sets for us all. Help us to be as willing to serve you with the opportunities that we are given. Amen

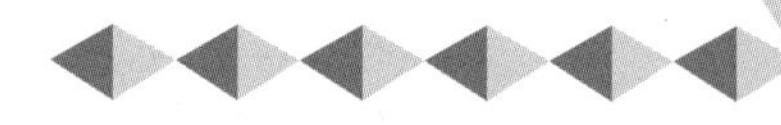

Activity areas

Small world play

Take the Mary, Joseph and angel figures from a nativity scene and create a home scene, perhaps in a cardboard box, where children can act out what happened between Mary and the angel.

Talk about how Mary must have felt when an angel suddenly appeared before her.

Role play / dressing up

Provide a selection of nativity costumes, particularly those used for Mary, Joseph and the angels. You will not need a baby Jesus doll for this activity. Draw attention to the roles of Mary and Gabriel at this stage of the story.

Talk about how this part of the story happened so much earlier than the rest of the Christmas story. At this point Mary had a lot to get used to and had no idea what would happen when Jesus was born!

Creative

Prepare a batch of salt dough, or provide some white air-drying clay, along with a selection of glitters and sequins and an angel-shaped cookie cutter. Invite the children to roll out the clay and cut out an angel shape, which they can then decorate with the sequins and glitter provided. Make a small hole in the top of the angel shape to enable a ribbon to be threaded through once the clay has hardened, so they can be hung from the Christmas tree.

Talk about where our ideas about angels come from; the Bible doesn't tell us very much about what they really look like. What do we think angels may look like?

Construction

Gather a supply of soft wood (such as balsa wood) in different-sized pieces, along with child-sized woodworking tools including saws, hammers, nails and sandpaper. Invite the children to use the tools provided (under supervision) to make something from the pieces of wood, encouraging free choice about what to make.

Talk about Joseph, a carpenter, to whom Mary was engaged. He was very surprised to discover that Mary was going to have a baby, but he took good care of her, and Jesus once he was born.

Books

Display a selection of nativity story books and other children's Bibles for the children to look at.

Support the children with their reading, as necessary, and talk about the way that the story unfolded after this episode.

Prayer and reflective activity

Provide a large piece of paper and marker pens and ask the children to think about different things that they can offer to God, in the same way that Mary did, writing or drawing their ideas on the paper.

Talk about the way that Mary willingly did as the angel asked. What opportunities do we have to put God first, just as Mary did?

Games

Games played today could include Chinese Whispers, as well as other games which involve passing on a message. The angel came to deliver an important message to Mary.

Story time

Today's retelling gives the children an opportunity to work together in pairs to perform the interaction between Mary and the angel, so invite those children who wish to participate to find a partner and decide upon their parts. Encourage the children to ad lib, miming and interacting with one another as you tell the story.

There once was a young lady called Mary, who came from a small town called Nazareth. She was engaged and was planning her wedding to a man called Joseph, who was a carpenter. One day, she was busy doing housework at home, tidying and cleaning the house, when suddenly, in front of her, there appeared an angel!

'Do not be afraid,' said the angel. 'I have a message for you from God!'

Mary listened to the angel as he told her that God had chosen her to have a special baby, God's son. She would have a baby boy, and she should name him 'Jesus'. Mary listened very carefully to everything that the angel said, then she told the angel she would do everything as God had said. It would be an honour for her!

It wasn't easy for Mary. She would need to tell Joseph what the angel had said, and then she would find herself getting ready to give birth far from home. But still, she did everything God said, knowing how precious it was to be used by him.

Prayer

Father God, thank you for the example that Mary gives us, doing what you asked of her and trusting in you. Help us to put you first, just as she did. Amen

Songs

Songs today could include:

- 'Mary's angel' (Niki Davies)
- 'Mary's song' (Richard Hubbard)

Take home

Encourage the children to take their angels home with them to put up as a decoration which reminds them of today's story and of the promise that Christmas is coming.

20
Jesus is born

For the team

Refer to pages 6–8 to see how the activity areas work together

Session theme

In this session, we celebrate one of our greatest and most well-known stories—the birth of Jesus. Through this session, we explore many of the well-known aspects of the story and find out more about the significance of each of these events.

Bible text: Luke 2:1–20

Team prayer

Father God, thank you that at this time of year we celebrate the gift of your Son, sent into our world. May we share our joy and excitement about this story with the children we meet and their families. Amen

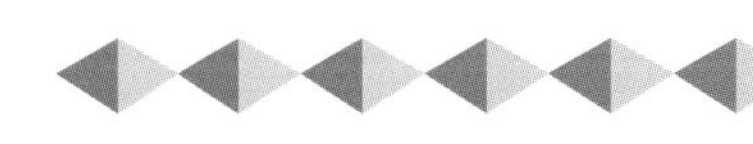

Activity areas

Small world play

Provide a selection of appropriate nativity scenes which the children can use to retell the story and to act out what happened that first Christmas.

Talk about the different stages of the story, as the children re-enact each element, and how the different nativity scenes that you have help us to understand different things about the story.

Role play / dressing up

Bring out the nativity costumes and invite the children to dress up as different characters in the story, perhaps retelling different parts of the story as they do so.

Talk about the different roles that different characters played in the nativity story.

Creative

Provide felt in different colours, glue, googly eyes, needle and thread and staplers and invite the children to create their own felt finger puppet of a nativity character of their choice. The basic puppet form can be put together by sewing or stapling the front and back sections, before glueing on the details.

Talk about the way that God included so many different people in the birth of his son, from poor shepherds, to wise men who had travelled from many miles away.

Construction

Set up a small gazebo and work with the children to transform it into a stable scene, draping fabric over the sides and setting up appropriate props, including a manger. Once complete, this could be combined with the role play activity so that children can dress up and act out what happened in the stable.

Talk about how strange the stable was to be the place where Jesus was born, not like our hospitals or cosy warm homes, and certainly not what Mary would have expected.

Writing

Provide a selection of Christmas cards or craft materials for the children to use to create their own. Invite the children to write a Christmas card, ready to send to a friend, with a message which shares a little of the nativity story.

Talk about the way that our friends and families celebrate Christmas, but lots of people don't know much about the story of the first Christmas. How can we find ways of sharing this important story with them?

Books

Set out a selection of children's Bibles and books retelling the nativity story. You may want to include other Christmas-themed books which include a focus on the nativity story.

Support the children in reading the books, where necessary, and discuss with them the things that interest them. You may find different details in each of the nativity story books which you can compare with one another.

Prayer and reflective activity

Have a number of small strips of paper ready, along with coloured pens and a stapler. Invite the children to write or draw a prayer on a strip of paper, before stapling them together to create a paper chain of prayers which can be hung around the room.

Talk about the children's prayer ideas as they write them down and discuss any issues raised through this activity.

Story time

Set up a large nativity scene which can be used during the retelling of the nativity story, beginning with an empty stable. For larger groups, provide a number of nativity sets which children can use together in small groups, manipulating the figures, and adding them to the scene as you retell the story. Children should be encouraged to share in the storytelling, contributing things that they remember as you tell this tale.

This is a story you might already know. Perhaps you can help me to retell the story.

When the time had nearly come for Mary to have her baby, she had to travel with Joseph to Bethlehem so that he could register for the census. They travelled for a long time, with a donkey, and when they reached Bethlehem, the town was very busy.

Joseph couldn't find anywhere for his family to stay, but a kind innkeeper let them stay in his stable. That night, the time came for Mary to have her baby. She named him Jesus, just as the angel had said, and laid him to rest in a manger.

Meanwhile, out on the hillside, some shepherds were caring for their sheep at night when suddenly, an angel appeared in the sky and told them about the new baby, who they would find safe in the stable in Bethlehem. Suddenly, the sky was filled with angels all singing and praising God.

The shepherds left their sheep and ran down to Bethlehem where they found the baby Jesus, lying in a manger in the stable, just as the angels had said. They worshipped the newborn baby, realising that he was very special.

Some time later some wise men came from many miles away in the east, bringing with them special gifts of gold, frankincense and myrrh.

This was no ordinary birth, and no ordinary baby. Mary knew she had been a part of something very special indeed.

Prayer

Lord Jesus, as we celebrate this special time of year, with family, food, presents and fun, help us to remember that we celebrate your birth and to thank you for coming to live among us. Amen

Songs

Songs today could include:

- 'Away in a manger' (Anon)
- 'Come and join the celebration' (Valerie Collinson)

Take home

Encourage the children to take some time out of the busy Christmas celebrations, to think about how they can remember the events of the first Christmas, and how we can give thanks for Jesus' birth. You may have some special Christmas events coming up which you could invite the children's families to join.

21

Jesus in the temple

For the team

Refer to pages 6–8 to see how the activity areas work together

Session theme

During this session, we take a glimpse at the otherwise secret childhood of Jesus, and think about what it means to grow spiritually, as well as physically, as a child of God.

Bible text: Luke 2:41–52

Team prayer

Lord Jesus, thank you for the example you set, through this story, as a child thirsty to learn more about God's kingdom. May we inspire the children with whom we work to learn more and to grow well as children of God. Amen

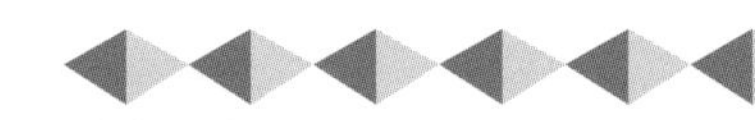

Activity areas

Role play / dressing up

Set up a classroom situation, perhaps with small tables and chairs, and a small black or white board, with chalk or dry-wipe pens that children can use to pretend to be the teacher, playing out scenarios that are familiar to them, from their own school experiences.

Talk about the different things that children do at school and how they learn. Jesus would not have gone to school as we know it, but he learned from his parents and the teachers at the temple, as he grew up.

Creative

Gather a selection of junk modelling and craft materials and invite the children to create their own model of the temple, as it would have been at the time of Jesus. (An internet search will provide pictures to help them do this.)

Talk about how the temple building would have been used at this time, as a place where people could learn more about God as well as coming together to worship him.

Construction

Provide a number of evenly sized cardboard boxes, wide masking tape or parcel tape and scissors and work together with the children to construct a large cardboard maze. Once complete, invite the children to work their way through the maze.

Talk about how Mary and Joseph must have felt when they first realised that Jesus was missing. Have any of the children ever got lost? How did they feel?

Writing

Provide a large piece of paper and felt pens. Invite the children to come and add their own 'big God questions', to the paper; things that they would like to ask God about.

Talk about the way that Jesus spent time in the temple asking the leaders important questions about God to help him to learn more. How can we find the answers to some of our questions?

Books

Provide a selection of children's story Bibles and books which retell this story, together with books which show what the temple may have looked like, and those which retell the story of the Passover festival.

Support the children in reading the books, where necessary, and discuss with them the things that interest them.

Prayer and reflective activity

Put up a height chart and invite each of the children to come and be measured, marking their height with a marker pen. As you do so, encourage the children to think about what it means to grow up and the changes that they have experienced already in life.

Talk about what it means to grow spiritually, emotionally and intellectually, as well as physically. The story today says that Jesus 'grew in wisdom and stature'. How can we do the same?

Games

Games played today could include hide and seek, as well as other games where someone or something is hidden, such as a treasure hunt.

Story time

This storytelling involves volunteers to play the parts of Jesus, Mary, Joseph and the teachers in the temple, miming or ad libbing as appropriate. The rest of the children could play the crowds of people, if you wish. Arrange the group with Mary and Joseph at one end of the room, and Jesus and the teachers at the other end. The rest of the children should sit or stand between them.

We don't know much about what happened to Jesus when he was growing up, but we do know this one story. Every year, Jesus and his parents went on a long journey to Jerusalem to celebrate the Passover festival. One year, something quite unusual happened. After the festival, Mary and Joseph set off for home, thinking that Jesus was walking with his friends. After a whole day of walking, they realised that Jesus wasn't with them at all, so they hurried back to Jerusalem to find out where he was.

Mary and Joseph should search for Jesus, looking through all the crowds of children and heading towards Jesus and the teachers.

After searching for Jesus for three days, they found him in the temple with the teachers, listening to what they had to say, and asking them questions about God. Everybody was surprised about how much Jesus knew; they were very impressed.

Encourage the volunteers to ad lib as appropriate.

Mary and Joseph were so glad to have found their son, but they wanted him to know that they were worried about him.

'But why?' asked Jesus. 'Didn't you know that I would be in my father's house?'

Jesus knew that he was God's son. As he grew up, he got ready to do God's work.

Prayer

Dear Jesus, thank you for the example you gave in the way you grew up, learning about what it meant to do things God's way. Help us to listen to those who help us to grow and follow you as we grow up too. Amen

Songs

Songs today could include:

- 'Father, we adore you' (Terry Coelho)

Take home

Encourage the children to think about the people they can share their 'big God questions' with, such as your own leaders, church leaders or family members. Follow this up in the coming weeks, encouraging the children to share what they are learning and what further questions they may have.

22
Jesus' baptism

For the team

Refer to pages 6–8 to see how the activity areas work together

Session theme

During this session, we discover more about a surprising encounter between Jesus and John the Baptist, see Jesus' obedience to his Father God, and get a glimpse of the unity of the Trinity. Through this session, we will relate the children's own experiences of baptism to the story of Jesus' own baptism.

Bible text: Matthew 3:13–17

Team prayer

Lord God, three-in-one, thank you for all that you are—so much more than we can really comprehend. May we not shy away from the more difficult stories that we read about in your book, but rather enjoy and share in the mystery of the events they describe. Amen

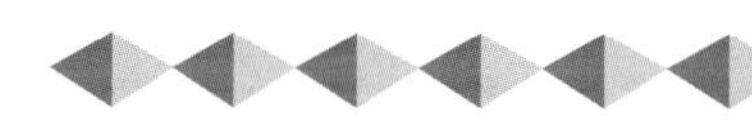

Activity areas

Small world play

Use a length of half drainpipe, sealed at either end to create a river, partially filled with water. Provide a selection of play figures and invite the children to act out today's story, with John standing in the water, and some people that he can 'baptise'.

Talk about how different Jesus' baptism was from the baptisms we may have seen or participated in, taking place in a river in the open air.

Role play / dressing up

Set up a 'home' setting, perhaps with chairs and tables, baby and crib, or a play kitchen and an appropriate selection of dressing-up items for the children to use. Invite the children to role play what it means to be a family, within the home setting you have created, assuming the roles of different family members.

Talk about what it means to be a family and explain that Jesus and John were cousins to one another.

Creative

Draw the outline of a dove shape on to thick paper or card (see template on page 125) and provide white feathers and PVA glue. Invite the children to help to complete the dove collage by covering the outline shape with white feathers.

Talk about the dove that appeared in the sky when Jesus was baptised, as a sign of the Holy Spirit.

Construction

Provide tin foil and challenge the children to construct a river shape, bending the foil up at the sides so that it will hold water without leaking.

Talk about the way that Jesus was baptised in the river. Some people today are still baptised in a river or in the sea, while many are baptised inside a church building.

Writing

Prepare some large paper question marks and pens, and invite the children to come and write their own 'baptism questions' on the question marks. These could relate to the story of Jesus' own baptism or to the children's own experiences of baptism. You could use the question marks to create a display of questions.

Talk about the children's questions as they write them down, and the ideas raised. How can the children find some of the answers to their questions?

Books

Set out a display of children's story Bibles and books which retell this story of Jesus' baptism. If possible, source a number of books about John the Baptist as well as books which show the landscape around the River Jordan.

Support the children in reading the books, where necessary, and discuss with them the things that interest them.

Prayer and reflective activity

Set out a selection of artefacts relating to baptism and how it is celebrated in your church tradition. If possible, you could also take the children to show them the font or baptistry pool which you use.

Talk about each of the artefacts; what each one means and how they are used. Encourage the children to share their own stories about baptism and what it means to them.

Story time

Today's retelling makes use of some simple fabric shapes to illustrate what happens in the story. For smaller groups, you could layer these shapes on top of one another on the floor in the centre of the group. For larger groups, you may prefer to create a board or banner which can be displayed at the front of the room. The props required are detailed as the script unfolds below.

Set out a neutral-coloured base in front of the children.

We heard, in our last story, about one of the things that happened to Jesus when he was a child. Today, we hear the first story about what happened to him when he was an adult, just beginning his work.

Jesus' cousin, John *(display a person outline on the background)* lived in the desert. He spent his days telling people about God and how people should live.

He often stood in the River Jordan *(add a strip of blue fabric to form a river, covering John's feet)*, calling people to turn their backs on the wrong way of living and to be baptised, as a sign that they wanted to follow God.

One day, Jesus came to the river *(add a second person outline)* and asked John to baptise him.

John was very surprised. He said that Jesus should baptise him, not the other way around! But John did exactly what Jesus asked of him.

As soon as Jesus was lifted out of the water, a white dove appeared in the sky *(place a white dove shape above Jesus)* as a sign of the Holy Spirit coming down upon Jesus, and God in heaven said; 'This is my son, I am very pleased with him.'

From this moment, Jesus began to do the work that he had come to earth to do.

Prayer

Lord Jesus, thank you that you were willing to work on earth to help us to understand what it means to be a follower of God. Help us to make you happy with the way that we choose to live. Amen

Songs

Songs today could include:

- 'Father, we adore you' (Terry Coelho)
- 'Let's make God happy' (Doug Horley)

Take home

Suggest that the children take some time to ask their own family members or friends about their baptism stories, perhaps sharing family photos or videos too.

23

Jesus chooses his disciples

For the team

Refer to pages 6–8 to see how the activity areas work together

Session theme

During this session, we will discover how Jesus invited some of the disciples to follow him and how that same invitation is extended to us, to follow him today.

Bible text: Matthew 4:18–22

Team prayer

Dear Jesus, thank you that you invite each of us to follow you, learning more about what it means to be a disciple, and to share your message with the people that we meet. Amen

Activity areas

Small world play

Set up a water tray with a variety of plastic toy boats which can float on the water, along with a number of small toy fish. Invite the children to experiment with the boats and fish to see which boats will remain afloat while holding the most fish.

Talk about how the first followers of Jesus were people who spent their days catching fish. They gave up the job and lifestyle they knew to follow Jesus.

Role play / dressing up

Set up a small boat, such as a dinghy, and fishing rods or nets, along with a large number of toy fish. Encourage the children to role play what the disciples would have done, trying to catch the fish in their nets, and gathering them in.

Talk about how, when Jesus told the disciples to put their nets into the water, they caught so many fish that they didn't know what to do with them all.

Creative

Lay out a length of paper on the floor and provide flat dishes of paint in a variety of colours. Invite the children to remove their shoes and socks before stepping in the paint and walking across the paper. You could also provide a few pairs of old wellington boots or shoes which children can wear to experiment with the footprints that they make. You will also need soap, water and towels to wash their feet afterwards.

Talk about the way that the disciples left what they were doing to follow Jesus, without hesitation or reluctance. What does it mean for us to follow Jesus?

Construction

Set up a magnetic fishing game for the children to have a go with, along with the materials needed for the children to work together to create their own version of the game. You will need card, paper clips, magnets, lengths of string and short wooden dowels. Work together with the children to create the game, before playing together.

Talk about what a change it would be for these fishermen to leave their nets and their jobs behind, to follow Jesus. What would it mean for them to be fishers of men?

Books

Provide a display of books, including children's story Bibles and books which retell the story, along with books about fish and fishing, perhaps those which show the way that the disciples would have worked at the time.

Support the children in reading the books, where necessary, and discuss with them the things that interest them.

Prayer and reflective activity

Hang up a large piece of paper and provide coloured paper, pens, scissors and glue. Provide smaller pieces of paper and invite the children to draw around their feet, before cutting out the shapes and writing their names on them. Create a display entitled 'We're following Jesus', with the foot shapes stuck on the paper in a line.

Talk about what it means for us to follow Jesus, as the first disciples did, learning from him and discovering more about the life that he wants us to live.

Games

Games played today could include Follow the Leader and other following or copying games, such as clapping games in which the children copy a rhythm clapped by a leader.

Story time

This story is told by a volunteer who plays the part of Simon, who should learn the script to perform, or ad lib, telling the story first-hand, perhaps sitting in the boat used for the role play activity.

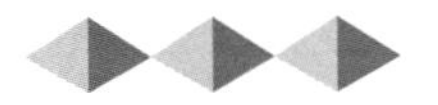

Have you heard about Jesus? He's causing quite a stir around here! I met him earlier today, it was such a strange experience! I can say one thing, I'll never be the same after meeting him.

You see, me and my friends had been out fishing all night, and it had been a really bad night too; we hadn't caught a single fish! So we sat here, earlier today, cleaning our nets and getting ready to try again later, when Jesus came by. He was busy teaching people about God, and there was quite a crowd listening to what he had to say. So Jesus asked us to take him out on to the lake, just a little way, so that he could carry on talking to the crowds who sat up here on the beach.

When we got out into the water, Jesus told us to put our nets back out into the lake. Well, it seemed like such a funny thing to say. We're the fishermen, after all, and even though we'd been out all night, we hadn't caught a single fish! But, you see, Jesus has something about him, and when he tells you to do something, you just want to do it.

So we put our nets down into the water and straight away we caught so many fish, our nets began to break! It was amazing! It was a bit of a struggle to get all the fish back to the shore! I'm glad there were so many people here listening to Jesus, because they saw what happened with all the fish too, and if they hadn't been here, I'm not sure anyone would have believed us!

Well, Jesus really had my attention then. How he could have known about the fish is beyond me; we've never caught that many fish before!

Then Jesus said the strangest thing. He asked us to leave our nets behind and stop being fishermen. 'Follow me,' he said, 'and I will make you fishers of men!'

Well, we weren't really sure what he meant by that, but Jesus really is such an interesting man, and here he was, inviting us to join him. So that's it, no more fishing for me. I'm off on a brand new adventure to see what Jesus has to show us. And just when the fishing was getting good!

Prayer

Dear Jesus, thank you that you invited Simon and his friends to follow you, and that you give us the same invitation. Help us to follow you always, learning more about you from the things that you say and do. Amen

Songs

- 'Come and join in the party' (Paul Field)

Take home

Suggest to the children that they could spend some time this week with somebody they know who is a Christian, asking them what it means to them to be a follower of Jesus.

24
The wise and foolish builders

For the team

Refer to pages 6–8 to see how the activity areas work together

Session theme

During this session, we explore one of the parables that Jesus told to help people understand what it meant to really trust in him. There is a direct challenge both to us, and to the children with whom we work, to build our lives on God's word as a firm foundation.

Bible text: Matthew 7:24–29

Team prayer

Dear Jesus, thank you that your stories still make sense to us today and still have messages to teach us. Help us to communicate what it means to build our lives with Jesus as a foundation and to explore practical ways that we can do this with the children in the group. Amen

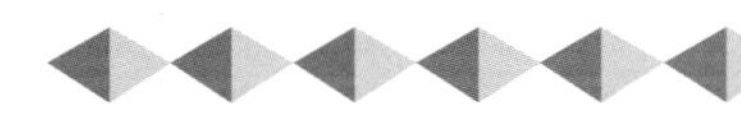

Activity areas

Small world play

Set up a tray with small piles of sand, gravel and small stones and provide a number of small toy vehicles as found on a building site. These could include diggers, rollers and lorries. Encourage the children to use the area as a building site, preparing the ground and building houses.

Talk about children's own experiences of watching these vehicles at work. House building nowadays is very different from when Jesus was telling this story. There were no powerful vehicles to use and people would have done all the work by hand.

Role play / dressing up

Provide a selection of high-vis vests, builders' helmets and play tools, such as hammers, saws, and so on, together with a number of large building blocks or cardboard boxes, which the children can use to role play working on a building site, building walls with the tools provided.

Talk about how hard builders work to make sure that the houses they build will last a long time. The man who built his house on the sand was careless and didn't think about what he was doing.

Creative

Gather some smooth pebbles and provide acrylic paints and paintbrushes. Invite the children to paint their own pebble as a reminder to trust God and build their life upon him. You may wish to provide painting aprons to protect the children's clothes from the acrylic paint.

Talk about the different images and words that the children decide to paint on their stones and why they have decided to use them.

Construction

Provide a number of building blocks and fill some shallow containers with different textures which can be used as a base for building upon. These could include chopped-up jelly, wet sand, dry sand and a piece of stone, and so on. Invite the children to experiment with building on each of these different surfaces to see what happens to each of their buildings.

Talk about the things that children notice as they build on each of the different surfaces. How does this help us to understand the story?

Books

Set out a display of books which retell this story, along with more of Jesus' parables, and children's Bibles. You could also display some books about houses, building and building sites.

Support the children in reading the books, where necessary, and discuss with them the things that interest them.

Prayer and reflective activity

Gather a selection of large building bricks and invite the children to write their name on one of the bricks, using a dry-wipe pen. Ask the children to help to build the bricks together to create a small model of a house.

Talk about the things that we depend on or trust in, such as our friends and family. What does it mean to depend on God even when we go through difficult situations?

Games

Source a selection of building, balancing or tumbling games, which the children can use to explore themes of building things up and seeing them fall down.

Story time

This story retelling involves all the children in performing simple hand actions at the appropriate times as they listen to the story. Invite all the children to sit on the floor with you and explain the actions, as detailed below, for them to practise before they need to use them in the story.

This is a story that Jesus once told to the crowds of people to help them to understand something important. Jesus said:

There once was a man who decided to build a house on a sandy beach.

Curl both hands to form fists and place them one on top of the other repeatedly, building tall towers in the air in front of you.

He finished building his house quickly, and when his work was done he settled himself down inside. Then the bad weather began. The rain came down.

Use your fingers to indicate raindrops, as you move your hands from above your head down to the ground.

The wind blew.

Use your hands to indicate wind blowing forward, from your mouth towards the centre of the room.

The flood waters rose.

Place your hands out in front of you, palms down at ground level, and use them to indicate flood waters rising, moving them slowly upwards and side to side as you do so.

And the house that was built on the sand crashed flat.

Clap your hands together loudly.

There was a second man who built a house on a firm foundation of rock.

Use your fists to build towers, as you did at the beginning of the storytelling.

He took his time, preparing good foundations and building a good, solid house. When he had finished building, he sat down, safe and secure inside his house. Then the rain began to fall.

Use your fingers to indicate raindrops, as you move your hands from above your head, down to the ground.

The wind blew.

Use your hands to indicate wind blowing forward, from your mouth towards the centre of the room.

The flood waters rose.

Place your hands out in front of you, palms down, at ground level, and use them to indicate flood waters rising, moving them slowly upwards and from side to side.

But the house that the man had built on the rock stood steady and firm and would not fall.

Jesus said that if we ignore the things that he said, then we are like the man who built on the sandy beach: his house did not last long. But if we pay attention to the things that he said, and live life his way, we are like the man who built his house on the solid rock, with a good, strong foundation for our lives.

Prayer

Dear Jesus, thank you for the things you said, which we can read about in the Bible. Please help us to build our lives on a firm foundation, and trust in the things you say. Amen

Songs

Songs today could include:

- 'I'm gonna build my life on solid rock' (Andrew and Pauline Pearson)
- 'The wise man built his house upon the rock' (Traditional)

Take home

Suggest that the children go out on a search for interesting buildings, perhaps taking photos of them to bring back to show the group, and think about the amount of time and effort that has gone into making those buildings safe and secure.

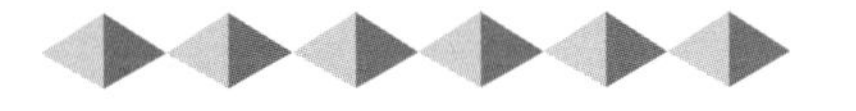

25
Jesus heals a paralysed man

For the team

Refer to pages 6–8 to see how the activity areas work together

Session theme

During this session, we explore one of the healing miracles of Jesus—a paralysed man whom Jesus completely healed. The theme of friendship is also explored, thinking about the determination of the man's friends to bring him to meet Jesus. An opportunity is given to think about how we can bring our friends to a place where they can encounter Jesus for themselves.

Bible text: Mark 2:1–17

Team prayer

Lord Jesus, thank you for your gift of healing and forgiveness, available to us all. Thank you, too, for the example of the man's four friends who knew that Jesus could transform their friend's life. Help us to find opportunities to bring our friends to meet Jesus for themselves. Amen

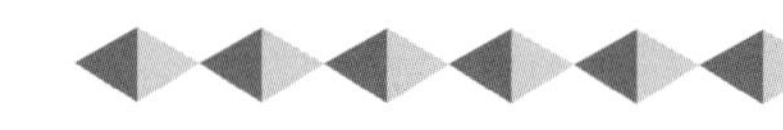

Activity areas

Small world play

Set up a small town scene with people figurines and flat-roofed houses made from building bricks which children can carefully dismantle to create a hole in the roof, and replay the way that the man's friends lowered him down into the house.

Talk about the way that large crowds followed Jesus to hear what he had to say. There are lots of stories in the Bible which talk about crowds of people, but these friends were determined to get close to Jesus.

Creative

Provide a number of plain pillow cases and fabric pens and invite the children to decorate their own pillow case to take home with them.

Talk about the way that the man in the story spent all his days lying down on his bed, until Jesus made him well again, and he could pick up all his things and take them away with him.

Construction

Before the session, prepare some plaster of Paris, setting a fairly thick layer in a tray-shaped mould, and tip it out when set. Provide some safe tools, such as teaspoons and clay-sculpting tools, and invite the children to try to chip into the plaster of Paris to make a hole in the centre.

Talk about the way that the man's friends had to dig into the roof to make a large hole, ready to lower the man through; because the house was so full, it was the only way they could get their friend close to Jesus. Ask the children why they think the men were so keen to get their friend close to Jesus; what difference did they think Jesus could make to his life?

Writing

Provide a selection of 'Get well soon' or 'Thinking of you' cards, or a selection of craft materials for the children to use to make their own, ready to send to a friend or family member who is unwell.

Talk about the men in the story who brought their friend to Jesus to be healed. Discuss any issues raised as the children create their cards, particularly questions or difficulties about the issue of healing. Also, use this as an opportunity to talk about how we can show that we care for our friends, just as the men in the story cared for their friend.

Books

Offer a selection of children's story Bibles and books which retell this and other stories about the miracles performed by Jesus. Other books could include stories that celebrate friendship.

Support the children in reading the books, where necessary, and discuss with them the things that interest them.

Prayer and reflective activity

Set up a display board with a person-shaped cut-out with 'Jesus' written on it. Provide a selection of smaller cut-outs, and invite the children to choose one, writing the name of one of their friends on it, before placing it close to Jesus.

Talk about the way that the men in the story wanted to bring their friend close to Jesus. What can we do to bring our friends close to Jesus? What would we like Jesus to do for them?

Games

Games which involve the children moving their whole bodies would work well for this session, perhaps including Simon Says, as a reminder of the way that the man in the story could move his whole body when Jesus had made him well again.

Story time

This story involves all the children in acting out what happens. You will need to choose volunteers to play the parts of the man, his four friends and Jesus. The rest of the children can play the crowds of people who had come to hear Jesus.

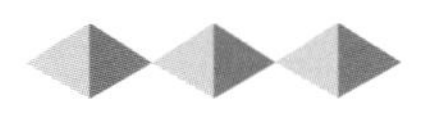

Everywhere that Jesus went, crowds of people travelled to see him and hear what he had to say. One day, while he was in somebody's house, the crowds were so big that the people filled the house and spilled out into the street.

Ask the children to gather around Jesus.

Suddenly, the crowds in the house could hear some scratching above their heads.

Encourage them all to look up.

Then little bits of the roof came down upon their heads.

Encourage the children to act appropriately.

Gradually, a hole appeared in the ceiling! And then, slowly, slowly a blanket was lowered down into the room, right in front of Jesus. On the blanket there lay a man, and above their heads were his four friends who had helped him down into the room.

Lay out the blanket at Jesus' feet, without trying to bring someone down from the roof!

Jesus looked at the man and saw just what he needed. 'Get up!' said Jesus. 'Pick up your mat and go home!' And do you know, that's exactly what the man did. Jesus also told the man that everything he had ever done wrong was forgiven. He had healed the man inside and out, and was giving him a new chance to start again, just as he does for us.

Prayer

Lord Jesus, thank you that you care for all people. Thank you that you can heal the sick, just as you did for the man in today's story. Today we pray for ... that you would be close to them and make them well again. Amen

Songs

Songs today could include:

- 'He's the man who calmed the sea' (Nick Harding)

Take home

Remind the children to take home the 'Get well soon' or 'Thinking of you' cards that they have made to pass on to a friend or family member. You could suggest that the children may wish to pray for the people they give the cards to as well.

26

The farmer and his seeds

For the team

Refer to pages 6–8 to see how the activity areas work together

Session theme

During this session, we explore another of Jesus' parables and think about how different people hear and respond to Jesus' teachings. As we share Jesus' message with the children in the group, it is easy to think that we know exactly how they will respond, but this story reminds us that the farmer knew nothing of the outcome of his work, simply that he needed to sow the seed.

Bible text: Mark 4:1–9, 13–20

Team prayer

Thank you, Jesus, for the stories you told which still speak to us today. As we think about the opportunities that we have to sow seeds into these children's lives, please go ahead of us, preparing them to be good soil, ready to accept your word. Amen

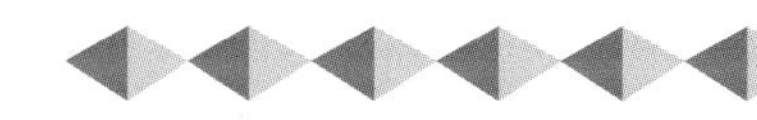

Activity areas

Small world play

Provide different trays filled with different types of soils along with gardening gloves to protect the children's hands and small trowels for the children to explore and experiment with. Try to represent the different soils mentioned in the parable for this sensory play.

Talk about what the children notice about each of the different soils as they play. Why do they think the seeds struggled in each of the different situations except the last?

Role play / dressing up

Gather a selection of appropriate dressing-up items and props which the children can use to role play being a gardener. Objects provided could include wellington boots, aprons, gardening gloves, plant pots, trowels and watering cans, etc.

Talk about the children's own experiences of helping to take care of a garden. What jobs do they need to do to help seeds to grow well?

Creative

Provide a selection of different seeds in a variety of colours, shapes and textures and invite the children to create their own textured seed picture. You could provide some simple line-drawn images which the children can use to glue different seeds in each segment of the picture, or invite them to create their own picture or pattern as appropriate.

Talk about the appearance of each of the different seeds that the children use in their pictures. The sower in the parable had many seeds to plant that day. I wonder if he paid close attention to them?

Construction

Provide a selection of craft materials, including different papers and cards, pipe cleaners, straws and playdough. Invite the children to create 'sculptures' to show what happened to the different seeds once they were planted, using the playdough to help their sculptures to stand up.

Talk about the ideas that children have for their sculptures, how they will represent the different seedlings and what each of them represents.

Books

Gather a selection of books about farming, seeds and plant-growing to display alongside appropriate children's Bibles and books which retell this parable.

Support the children in reading the books, where necessary, and discuss with them the things that interest them. Talk about how the books help us to understand this parable better.

Prayer and reflective activity

Provide small plant pots, compost and seeds and invite the children to plant a seed in a pot ready to take home with them.

Talk about the different 'seeds' that people have planted in the children's own lives when they have told them about Jesus. When they take their seedling home and watch it grow, encourage the children to use it as a reminder to think about how their relationship with Jesus is growing too.

Games

Create a set of actions for the children, as reminders of the different soil types in the story. For instance, when you say 'good soil', the children should all stand up straight and tall, and when you say 'rocky pathway', the children could pretend to be birds pecking at the ground.

Story time

Ask the children to bring out their 'sculptures', as created in the construction activity, to use during this story retelling. Ask the children to sit together and to bring their sculptures to the front of the group at the appropriate points in the story. You may need to remind the children to do so as you tell the story.

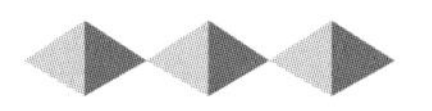

There once was a farmer who had a great big bag of seed to sow.

The first seeds that he scattered fell on the pathway. Those seeds couldn't grow at all. Along came the birds and pecked up all the seeds straight away!

Some of the seeds fell on the rocky soil. To begin with, they grew well, but when the sun came out it scorched the plants and they died, because they had not grown good roots under the soil.

More of the seeds fell where the thorn bushes grew. They also grew to begin with, but the thorns choked the little plants, and they too died.

Finally, some of the seeds fell on good soil where they grew good, strong roots deep into the soil and good strong stems up to the sunshine.

Jesus explained to the crowds of people that this was a story about what happens when we listen to the things that he says. Some people don't listen at all, and like the seeds on the pathway, those teachings get swallowed up straight away.

Some people listen to begin with, but because they don't let Jesus' teaching go down deep within them, they do not really learn anything either.

Other people are like the thorn bushes. They are too easily distracted by their worries and do not really listen to Jesus.

Finally, people who really listen to the things that Jesus has to say grow well, like the seeds set in good soil, firm and strong and trusting in Jesus.

The question for the crowds who listened to Jesus that day is the same as for us today; what type of soil are we?

Prayer

Dear Jesus, thank you that someone took time to sow seeds into our own lives. Help us to be good soil, where our relationship with you can grow. Amen

Songs

Songs today could include:

- 'Sow 'n' sow' (Ian Smale)

Take home

Remind the children to take home their planted seeds from the prayer and reflective activity, or provide seeds for the children to take home to plant. As they watch their plants grow, encourage them to think about this story and the way that we grow when we listen to Jesus.

27

Jesus feeds 5000 people

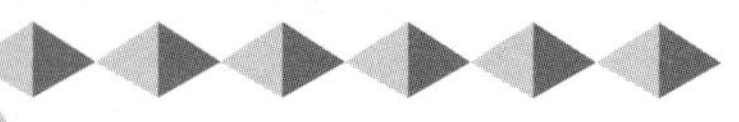

For the team

Refer to pages 6–8 to see how the activity areas work together

Session theme

In this session, we discover another of Jesus' miracles and consider how he can use the tiny gifts that we bring back to him and multiply them for the benefit of many. This session reminds us all that no matter how small we think our offerings are, Jesus can use them when we give them willingly to him.

Bible text: Mark 6:30–44

Team prayer

Dear Jesus, thank you that even though you have power and authority over all things, you still choose to work together with us to transform the world. Please take our gifts of serving these children and multiply them to achieve great things in their lives. Amen

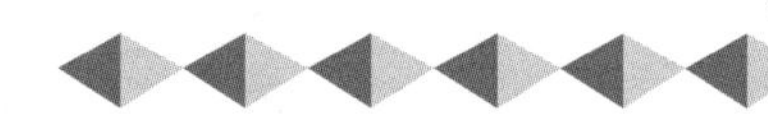

Activity areas

Small world play

Form a green 'grassy' hill, perhaps using a large piece of green fabric draped over piles of books, and provide people figurines, tiny baskets and picnic blankets which children can use to re-enact the way that Jesus used what little food there was to feed the huge crowds.

Talk about how surprising this story is and how different this would have been from a normal family picnic lunch.

Role play / dressing up

Set up a small kitchen scene with play food or playdough and a selection of kitchen utensils, aprons, a cool box and plastic plates, etc. Invite the children to play setting up a picnic, as though they were packing it ready to take out for the day.

Talk about the young boy in the story who had brought his lunch with him. Where do you think he was going when he left home that morning? How would his mother feel when she found out about the way he shared his lunch that day?

Creative

Provide a range of different sliced bread and bread rolls as well as tuna mixed with either mayonnaise or vinegar and invite the children to make their own tuna sandwiches. (Remember to check for food allergies.)

Talk about the children's favourite sandwich fillings. The day that Jesus fed the 5000, people had no choice about what they would eat because only one person actually had any food with them.

Construction

Provide a selection of materials such as canes, straws (plastic and paper), willow and reeds, which the children can use to experiment with weaving. You may be able to source a basket weaving kit which the children can use instead.

Talk about the way that there were twelve baskets of leftovers, after everyone had eaten what they wanted. What a miracle Jesus had performed!

Books

Books offered today should include children's Bibles, and story books which retell the story of this and other miracles performed by Jesus.

Support the children in reading the books, where necessary, and discuss with them the things that interest them.

Prayer and reflective activity

Place an open lunch box on the table and provide pieces of paper and pens. Invite the children to write or draw a picture of something they have which they can share, just like the boy in the story who shared his lunch with Jesus, and to put it into the lunch box.

Talk about the different things that children put into the lunch box. How can we share these things with other people? How can Jesus use the things that we offer to him?

Games

You could set out a magnetic fishing game for the children to play with today, perhaps encouraging them to match pairs of fish, as a reminder of the two fish in today's story.

Story time

This story retelling uses simple felt shapes, which will need to be prepared before the session, to build up a picture as you tell the story. The images you will need are detailed below. Ask the children to sit down with a green felt board displayed at the front of the group, ready to build as you tell the story.

Everywhere Jesus went, crowds of people followed him, wanting to hear more of the important things he had to tell them.

As you say this, add a number of felt people shapes to the board, in assorted colours, to represent the crowd. Slightly to one side, position a white figure to represent Jesus.

One day, Jesus had spent a whole day talking to the crowds about God and his love for them. There were so many people—at least 5000 of them! It was getting late and the people needed to go home so they could have some dinner, but Jesus told the disciples to find them something to eat there.

Add a few people shapes around Jesus to represent the disciples.

The disciples had no food with them, and the crowds were so large that they would need a lot of food! But Jesus told them to see what they could find. The disciples found one young boy with a tiny picnic; just five small loaves of bread and two small fish.

Place a smaller person shape near to Jesus, and close to him position the bread and fish shapes.

This was only enough food to feed the boy, but Jesus knew what he could do. He told the disciples to organise the crowds into smaller groups.

Reposition the people shapes on the board, arranging them in smaller groups.

Then he prayed over the tiny picnic that he had. He told the disciples to share the food with the people and to make sure that everyone had what they wanted.

As you say this, put out more bread and fish shapes in the middle of each group of people.

The disciples were amazed! They passed the food around the crowds of people, but there was no sign of the food running out.

Once everyone had finished eating, Jesus told the disciples to gather up the leftovers. Everyone had plenty of food to eat and, remarkably, there were twelve baskets of food left over!

As you say this, remove the fish and bread roll shapes and place twelve basket shapes on the board.

Prayer

Dear Jesus, thank you for this story, which reminds us that you care for all your people and give us everything we need. Help us to listen to the things you teach, just as the crowds listened to you. Amen

Songs

Songs today could include:

- '5000 + hungry folk' (Ian Smale)

Take home

Suggest to the children that they take out of the lunch box the piece of paper that they put into it, as a reminder of the thing they want to offer back to God.

28
The good Samaritan

For the team

Refer to pages 6–8 to see how the activity areas work together

Session theme

This session explores one of Jesus' most well-known parables, and discovers what it really means to show love to all people, regardless of race, status or background, following the example of the good Samaritan in the story.

Bible text: Luke 10:25–37

Team prayer

Father God, forgive us for the times when we forget that we are all your children, known and loved by you. Help us to share that unconditional love with all people. Amen

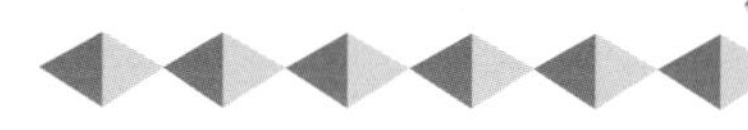

Activity areas

Small world play

Set up a small hospital or doctor's surgery scene with the appropriate play figures and related props for the children to act out how people care for those who are sick.

Talk about the children's own experiences of being unwell and visiting a doctor. How did they make them feel better?

Role play / dressing up

Provide a selection of different bandages and dressings and work with the children to 'dress' different wounds on one another, wrapping up the limbs as the children choose to do so. If you have any qualified first aiders in the group, they could use this time to teach some basic first aid to the children.

Talk about the way that you wrap the 'wounds', and how the good Samaritan took care of the wounds of the injured man in the story.

Creative

Provide a selection of craft materials, including coloured card, scissors, glue and a range of collaging materials. Invite the children to create a 'Get well soon' or 'Thinking of you' card for someone they know who is unwell or feeling down.

Talk about the different issues that this activity raises for the children as they make their cards. How can we be a good Samaritan, by helping to make other people feel better?

Construction

Provide a selection of junk modelling materials and invite the children to work together with you to create a 'junk model' donkey. Challenge the children to make sure that the donkey can stand up independently when it is complete.

Talk about the way that the Samaritan scooped the injured man on to the back of his donkey to take him to a place where he could be looked after.

Books

Set out a display of books about people who help us, along with children's Bibles and story books which retell this and other parables.

Support the children in reading the books, where necessary, and discuss with them the things that interest them.

Prayer and reflective activity

Hang up a large piece of paper and provide a selection of newspapers and magazines, together with scissors and glue. Invite the children to cut out pictures of different people to create a collage, including people of different races, genders, ages, physical appearances, and so on.

Talk about the great diversity in the human race and how we can celebrate God's great creation. We are all God's children and he wants us all to feel included and loved in his family.

Games

There are a number of appropriate board games that you could set up to support the theme for this session, including those games based on themes of doctors or hospitals, as well as games that involve donkeys.

Story time

This story retelling uses volunteers to act out what happened, as you narrate. You will need somebody to play the part of the victim, a small group to play the robbers, a priest, a temple helper, the Samaritan and an innkeeper. You could also provide a selection of simple costumes and props, including a hobby horse, bandages and a bag of coins. This retelling could be rehearsed in advance, or simply ask the volunteers to step up and mime appropriately at the relevant point in the story.

A teacher once visited Jesus to ask him more about what it means to show love to our neighbours. He was hoping that Jesus would give an easy answer, but Jesus challenged him to think about the people we really show love to. Jesus told the teacher this story…

There once was a man who was travelling along a road, on his own, when suddenly a group of robbers jumped out and attacked him! They hurt the man and took all the things he was carrying away with them, leaving him lying on the road.

Sometime later, a priest was travelling along the road. You might expect the priest to stop and help an injured man, but he didn't. He crossed the road and walked right past the man, leaving him lying on the road.

Sometime later, a temple helper was walking along the road. You might expect a man who worked in God's temple to stop and help an injured man, but he didn't. He crossed the road and walked past the man, leaving him lying on the road.

Sometime later, a Samaritan was walking along the road. Now, everybody knows that a Samaritan wouldn't stop to help a Jewish man. These two groups of people really hated each other and would never show love to one another.

But the Samaritan did stop. He bandaged the injured man's wounds and helped him up on to a donkey. Then the Samaritan led him to an inn where he gave the innkeeper money to help him to take care of the man. He even promised to come back in a few days to see how the man was, and to pay for any further care he might need.

So Jesus asked the teacher, 'Who do you think acted like a neighbour?' He wanted the teacher, and us, to understand that everybody can be our neighbour, no matter where they come from, what they look like or who they are. We can show love to everyone we meet.

Prayer

Dear Jesus, thank you for the stories you told that help us to understand important ideas. Help us to be good neighbours, showing love to the people we meet and know, whether they are like us or very different from us, because you love all people. Amen

Songs

Songs today could include:

- 'Jerusalem to Jericho' (Ian Smale)

Take home

Remind the children to take home the 'Get well soon' and 'Thinking of you' cards that they have made, ready to pass on to their friends or family members. They may wish to do something else, together with their family, to show love to those people, perhaps offering a gift or doing something practical to help, as a good neighbour.

The lost sheep

For the team

Refer to pages 6–8 to see how the activity areas work together

Session theme

This is the first in a series of three sessions exploring Jesus' lost and found parables. In this session, we discover a good shepherd who searched high and low for his missing sheep, reminding us of God's love for those who are missing from his family.

Bible text: Luke 15:4–7

Team prayer

Father God, thank you that just like the good shepherd who searched for his missing sheep, you search for your children until they are safely home with you. Help us to share your great love for the children we work with today. Amen

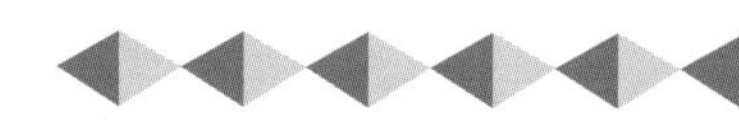

Activity areas

Small world play

Set up a farmyard scene with a selection of farm animals, including sheep, along with a shepherd, some sheepfolds and a sheepdog. Invite the children to play with the farm scene, drawing particular attention to the shepherd and sheep.

Talk about the way a shepherd takes care of the sheep on a farm, as they show this through their play. What special jobs and responsibilities does the shepherd have to keep the sheep safe and give them what they need?

Role play / dressing up

This activity could be combined with the game suggested today. Provide an appropriate selection of dressing-up items, such as wellington boots, jackets and caps and shepherds' crooks or walking sticks that can be used as a crook. You could also provide a toy sheepdog and a number of sheep for the children to use to role play herding the sheep, or hunting for the lost sheep, as in the game activity below.

Talk about the different jobs that shepherds do to care for their sheep. What does it mean for God to be a good shepherd?

Creative

Prepare a batch of salt dough and provide a selection of clay-moulding tools which the children can use to create a model of a sheep. A garlic press can be used to create a woolly sheep's coat, or patterns can be carved into the dough using clay tools.

Talk about what the children already know about sheep and what care they need. Ask the children how well they think a farmer would have known his sheep; could he tell them apart by their markings? What else do you think he would have known about them?

Construction

Provide a construction set, either with interlocking sections or with nuts and bolts, and challenge the children to build a model sheep-pen which can house some toy sheep securely.

Talk about the way that a sheep-pen is used to gather the sheep together to keep them safe. When the sheep were all in the pen, the shepherd would know if any of them were missing.

Books

Display a selection of books which retell this and other parables, alongside children's Bibles. Other books provided could include books about sheep and farming and stories with a theme of lost and found.

Support the children in reading the books, where necessary, and discuss with them the things that interest them.

Prayer and reflective activity

Cut out some simple sheep shapes from card, and invite the children to choose one to decorate, writing their own name on to it. Provide a small cardboard pen, and invite the children to put their sheep into the pen. If they wish to do so, they can also write the name of their friends on the sheep before putting them in the pen.

Talk about what it means to be taken care of by Jesus, held close by him and protected from harm. Remind the children that our friends can make their own choice about whether they want to follow Jesus, but we can pray for them, that we would have the opportunity to tell them about Jesus.

Games

Hide some sheep (either printed pictures or small toys) around the room before the session begins and invite the children to hunt for the pictures, before gathering the sheep together to count. Can the children find all the lost sheep?

Story time

Invite all the children to play a part in this story, playing the parts of the sheep. The story should be told by a confident leader, in the role of shepherd, who should learn or ad lib the script as appropriate. Another leader needs to play the part of the lost sheep, discreetly hiding at the appropriate point. Any children uncomfortable with participating should be allowed to sit and observe. It may work well to limit the space used by the children to ensure that it does not take too long to find them.

Ooh, I do love being a shepherd. Every day, out in the sunshine, looking after my sheep. There you go, Molly, have some food! Billy, budge up a bit, you're squashing the lambs there!

Interact with the children as appropriate.

Now then, my lovelies, you've got all this space in this lovely grassy meadow, you don't need to sit by me. Spread out, eat the grass and enjoy this sunny day. Don't worry, I'll keep you safe and tonight I'll bring you all back home, safe and sound.

Encourage the children to spread out around the room, miming appropriately, and ad lib further interactions with them before pausing for a moment, perhaps sitting down for a rest.

Ah now, it's getting late, I'd better get my lovely lambs back home, safe and sound.

Gather the sheep into a group in the centre, perhaps in a follow-the-leader fashion, as you call their names.

Right, come along, Larry; and you, Flower. Ewan and Shaun, in you come.

Process all the children together to a small space at one side of the room.

Here we are now, everybody safely home, all 99 of you. Hang on… I don't have 99 sheep… I have 100 sheep. I've lost one! Right, you sheep, you stay here, safe and sound, and I'll go back and find that missing one.

The leader playing the lost sheep should now be hidden somewhere. Involve the children in trying to find the lost one, while staying in their safe space. Then bring the lost sheep safely home and encourage the children to cheer and celebrate together.

Say that Jesus once told a story just like this to help us to understand just how much he loves us and cares for us. He said that whenever one person chooses to follow him, the angels in heaven have a party because they are so glad that we are safe and sound.

Prayer

Father God, thank you that you love each of us and care for us, just as a good shepherd cares for his sheep. Please help us to stay close to you, and to tell other people that you love them too. Amen

Songs

Songs today could include:

- 'God is my shepherd' (Jim Bailey)

Take home

As children leave this session, you could suggest that they visit a local farm where they can see sheep for themselves and watch the way they are cared for by the shepherd.

30 The lost coin

For the team

Refer to pages 6–8 to see how the activity areas work together

Session theme

This is the second in a series of three exploring Jesus' lost and found parables. During this session, we discover how God sees value in each of us, just as the woman in the story valued her missing coin and searched high and low until it was found.

Bible text: Luke 15:8–10

Team prayer

Father God, thank you that we are all known, valued and loved by you. Help us to share this truth with the children we work with today, that they may know how precious they are to you. Amen

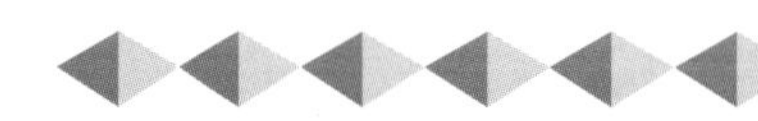

Activity areas

Small world play

Set up a doll's house, with some dolls that the children can play with, along with small brushes and soft dusting cloths which can be used to role play cleaning and tidying the house.

Talk about the way the woman in the story cleaned her house from top to bottom, searching for her lost coin. Ask the children if they have ever lost something that was precious to them. Where did they have to hunt for it? How did they feel when it was found again?

Role play / dressing up

Before the session, hide a number of small coins—real, plastic or chocolate—around the room. Invite the children to play the role of the woman in the story and to hunt for the missing coins.

Talk about how much fun the children have hunting for the coins. The woman in the story only lost one coin, but it was very precious to her and she searched high and low to find it.

Creative

Collect a number of empty glass jars (with lids) before the session. Using a sharp knife, carefully cut a small slit in each lid, large enough for coins to go through. Provide a selection of stickers and invite the children to decorate their own coin jar, which can be used as a money box.

Talk about how we can keep our money safe, in a purse or money box or at the bank. Where do you think the woman in the story kept her money?

Construction

Gather a number of coins, perhaps only pennies, and challenge the children to see how tall a tower they can build, counting the coins as they do so, before the coin tower topples down.

Talk about the woman in the story. She had ten coins and they were very precious to her.

Books

Set out a display of books including children's Bibles and story books which retell this story, along with stories with a theme of lost and found.

Support the children in reading the books, where necessary, and discuss with them the things that interest them.

Prayer and reflective activity

Before the session, hide one coin in the room. This could be a real penny, an enlarged picture or a chocolate coin. On the signal to begin, everybody should work together to find the one missing penny. When it is found, invite the children to celebrate with you, perhaps enjoying cakes and a drink together, sharing in a small party.

Talk about how it feels to participate in the story, as the woman did. Why do we want to celebrate once the coin is found? How does this help us to understand the story?

Games

A number of different board games are available which use coins, including piggy bank games or shopping games. Any games with these themes would work well at this session.

Story time

Prepare for today's story by sticking ten plastic or foil coins on to the fingers of a pair of gloves. Ask the children to sit down with you, in a position where they can see your hands.

There once was a woman who had ten silver coins.
Wriggle your fingers to show the coins.

She kept them safe within her home, only taking them out to polish them.

One day the woman took her coins out to polish—but first she counted them.
Raise your fingers one at a time as you count them, but keep one finger or thumb folded down.

1, 2, 3, 4, 5, 6, 7, 8, 9. There were only nine of her coins in her hand.

The woman was very worried about her missing coin. It was very precious to her. So she searched her house, high and low, sweeping the floor and checking the shelves, looking all over the house until she found the missing coin.

Eventually she did find the coin. Perhaps it was hidden under a rug, or had slipped down between the floorboards. But she was so happy when she found the missing coin: 1, 2, 3, 4, 5, 6, 7, 8, 9, 10!

All her coins were safely back together in one place. The woman was delighted! So happy, in fact, that she held a party and invited all her neighbours round to celebrate with her that the coin that she had lost was now found.

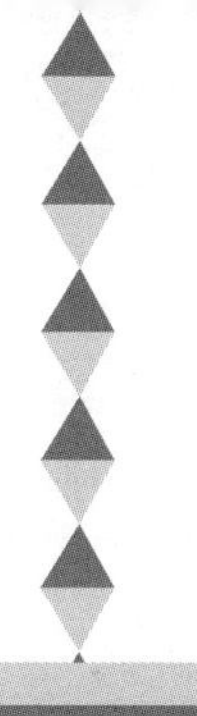
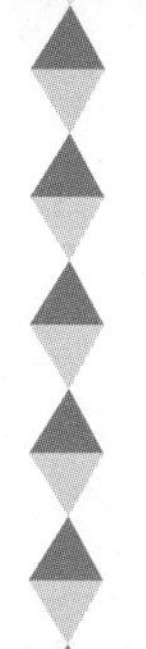

Jesus said that when one of us comes back to him, and chooses to be his friend, it is just like that. The angels in heaven have a party because someone who was lost has been found again, safe and sound.

Prayer

Father God, thank you that you love us all so very much and that when we come back to you, you celebrate that we are in your family. Help us to tell other people that you love them too, and help them to find their way back to you. Amen

Songs

Songs today could include:

- 'Singing with the angels' (Sarah Pickering)
- 'Ten silver coins' (Ian Smale)

Take home

Give each of the children a chocolate coin and suggest that they may wish to find someone to give the coin to, sharing today's story with them as they do so.

31
The prodigal son

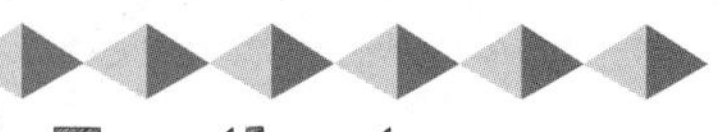

For the team

Refer to pages 6–8 to see how the activity areas work together

Session theme

In this final session in the trilogy of lost and found stories, we explore the unconditional love of God the Father towards us his children, and consider how we can respond to this great gift.

Bible text: Luke 15:11–32

Team prayer

Father God, thank you for loving us all the same, whether we stay by your side or travel far from home. May we celebrate with you when your children come back home.

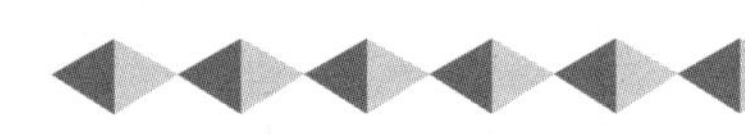

Activity areas

Small world play

Set up a farmyard scene for this session and ensure that the animals you provide include toy pigs.

Talk about the different jobs that farmers do to take care of their animals and the different animals that you would find on a farm. Which animals would the children like to take care of? What do you think is the worst job on a farm? The son in the story had to look after the pigs, and everyone thought that was the worst job.

Role play / dressing up

Set up a party scene, perhaps with a party table, paper plates and cups, along with pretend food. Hang party banners and balloons around this area and provide party hats for the children to wear. You could also provide some music and a few simple party games with some small prizes.

Talk about the children's own experiences of going to parties and the different reasons why we have parties. Remind the children that the father in the story held a big party to celebrate when his son came back home.

Creative

Provide a selection of magazines and newspapers, as well as paper, glue and scissors. Invite the children to create a collage of faces depicting different emotions.

Talk about the diverse emotions felt by the characters at the different stages in the story. How might we relate to the emotions of each of the central characters as the story is told?

Construction

Gather a large quantity of newspapers and rolls of masking tape, and invite the children to help you to construct a pen to keep the pigs in. You will need to roll the newspapers to make sticks first, which can then be assembled to make a pig pen.

Talk about how the son in the story had to look after the pigs, when all his money had gone, and how this was considered the worst job he could have had.

Writing

Offer paper and a selection of pens and pencils for the children to use to create a 'Missing' poster, on behalf of the father in the story. They could draw a picture of the missing son and write a few descriptive phrases, as they imagine how the son would look.

Talk about how the father must have felt when his son left home and how, over time, he missed his son more and more.

Books

Display a variety of children's Bibles and books telling the story of the prodigal son, alongside books about families and pigs.

Support the children in reading the books, where necessary, and discuss with them the things that interest them.

Prayer and reflective activity

Prepare a 'mucky' bowl filled with things for the children to handle that will make their hands dirty, such as sand or cornflour and water, coffee granules or tea, custard or jelly. (Remember to check for allergies.) You will also need a second bowl of water and soap, a sponge and a hand towel. Invite the children to dip their hands into the mucky bowl to make them messy, before washing their hands clean.

Talk about the fact that the son would have been very messy when he got home after looking after the pigs. Just like the son in the story, when we do things that mess us up on the inside, God can wash us clean and give us a fresh start, when we say sorry for the things that we do wrong.

Games

Games played today could include Hide and Seek, Squeak Piggy Squeak, and scavenger hunts, perhaps for symbols related to the story.

Story time

Today's story is told dramatically and will need some volunteers to help. You will need children to play the father, his two sons, a few partygoers and some pigs. Explain that they should mime appropriately, and repeat the appropriate words as you tell the story. Provide a bag of coins, a cloak, a ring and some party blowers or party poppers to be used at appropriate points.

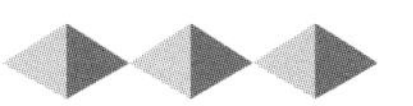

This is a story that Jesus told about a farmer and his two sons, whom he loved very much. One day, the younger son said to his dad, 'One day, I will be given half of all your money but I don't want to wait. I want it now! Give me my share of the money so that I can go off and explore the world.' What an unkind thing to say!

His dad was very sad, but he did give his son the money; so off he went to explore the world. At first, he enjoyed his new adventure on his own, spending all his money and making lots of new friends. He went to lots of parties, bought expensive things and felt very happy. But when the money ran out, his new friends disappeared too, and he soon found himself with no friends, no money, no home and no food.

He found a job looking after smelly pigs! He was so poor and hungry that he wanted to eat the pig food. This made him stop and think; he knew that his dad took better care of the men who worked on his farm than this. Perhaps he should go back home and say sorry.

So the boy went back home to his dad, and on the way home he thought about what he should say to his dad to tell him how sorry he was. But when he got home, he didn't have a chance to say a thing because his dad, who had been looking out for him, ran out to give him a big hug and tell him how much he loved him. Then his dad threw a great big party to celebrate his son coming back home.

Blow the party blowers and pop the party poppers.

The older son couldn't understand why his dad wasn't angry with his brother. So his dad explained, 'I love both of you very much and now you are both back home with me; that makes me feel very happy!'

God is like the dad in that story and he loves us all as his children; I wonder how that makes you feel?

Prayer

Thank you, God, that you love us, like a perfect dad loves his children. Thank you that we can be a family because of your gift of love. Amen

Songs

Songs today could include:

- 'Father God I wonder' (Ishmael)

Take home

Suggest that the children have a little party at home to celebrate being a family together. This could be something small like decorating cupcakes together or perhaps sharing a special meal.

32

Jesus notices Zacchaeus

For the team

Refer to pages 6–8 to see how the activity areas work together

Session theme

This session tells the story of a surprising encounter between Jesus and Zacchaeus and discovers how Zacchaeus would be forever changed by that one meeting. We will think about how our own lives can be changed as a result of meeting Jesus, and how he calls us to live differently.

Bible text: Luke 19:1–10

Team prayer

Dear Jesus, thank you for changing our lives and giving us a fresh start. Help us to remember your transforming power in our own lives and to share the hope that this gives with the children we work with today. Amen

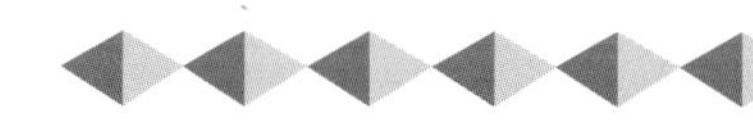

Activity areas

Small world play

Prepare a street scene, with different buildings and a selection of play figures representing a wide selection of people—different ages, races, disabilities, and so on—for the children to play with.

Talk about the way we make decisions about people and how we feel about them as soon as we meet them. How do we make these decisions? Which of the play figures do you think Jesus would most want to spend time with? Jesus surprised everyone when he chose to speak to Zacchaeus.

Role play / dressing up

Set up a tea party scene, perhaps around a table with appropriate refreshments, such as small sandwiches, cakes, biscuits and drinks. Play food could be used as an alternative.

Talk about how Jesus told Zacchaeus he would be coming to his house for tea. Zacchaeus would not have had time to set up a special meal, but it didn't matter. Jesus just wanted to spend time with him.

Creative

Provide a selection of papers and other craft materials, along with pens, scissors and glue for the children to use to create an invitation, perhaps to give to a friend of theirs to invite them to come to this group, or to a special event you may be running. You could provide template wording for the children to use or a template invitation for them to decorate.

Talk about the way that Jesus often spent time with the people who were unexpected or surprising because they weren't the popular, important people. Jesus wants to get to know us and our friends too. How can we help him to get to know us?

Construction

Work together with the children to construct a large model tree, using a selection of branches, sticks and leaves. If appropriate, take the children out into the local environment to gather for themselves the materials they will need.

Talk about the way that Zacchaeus climbed into the tree to get a better view of Jesus and discuss the children's own experiences of tree climbing.

Books

Books offered today should include children's Bibles and story books which retell the story of Zacchaeus, as well as other stories about people who met Jesus.

Support the children in reading the books, where necessary, and discuss with them the things that interest them.

Prayer and reflective activity

Set up a table, perhaps with a tablecloth, and two chairs. Invite the children to come and sit at the table and to think about what they might say to Jesus if they sat opposite him at a table, just as Zacchaeus did.

Talk about the children's ideas of what they might talk to Jesus about. What do you think he might say to them? What would they like to say to Jesus?

Games

Play a game in which the children are challenged to give things away. For example, each player might have a handful of buttons or coloured beads and try to pass them on to the other players as quickly as possible. The winner would be the person to give away all their buttons first, as a reminder of the way that Zacchaeus gave away his money.

Story time

Today's story is performed as an interview between two leaders, one asking the questions, and the other playing the part of Zacchaeus, who could be seated on a chair. The interviewer could hold a large microphone prop. The story would work particularly well if the leaders could learn the script and perform it as though simply talking to one another.

Interviewer: Hello and welcome to our special visitor, Zac.

Zacchaeus: It's Zacchaeus, actually.

Interviewer: I'm sorry, Zacchaeus. Welcome to our group, thanks for coming. We hear you have a story to tell us, about what happened when you met Jesus?

Zacchaeus: That's right. It really was such a special day. I heard that Jesus was coming to town. Everybody wanted to see him, me too! There were such big crowds in the town that day. Well, you can see that I'm not the tallest of men, and nobody was going to get out of my way so I could get a glimpse of him.

Interviewer: Are you not very popular then, Zacchaeus?

Zacchaeus: You could say that! I haven't always treated other people very well, you see. I work for the Romans. It's my job to take the taxes from people to pay the bills. That would make me unpopular enough, but I'm afraid I haven't always been a very good man. I used to take extra money and keep it for myself, you see.

Interviewer: Oh Zacchaeus, that is bad.

Zacchaeus: I know, but all that's changed now, since I met Jesus that day. You see, because I'm so short, I climbed up into a tree to get a better view as Jesus walked past. Then he came walking down the street, surrounded by so many people who wanted to meet him, but when he got close to the tree that I was sitting in, he stopped walking and looked up, straight at me! Then he said: 'Zacchaeus, come down, I'm coming to your house for tea!' The other people didn't like that. They thought he should go to someone who is good and kind for tea, but Jesus was quite sure.

Interviewer: So what happened then?

Zacchaeus: I took Jesus back to my house. It was a bit untidy, and I didn't have anything special in for tea, but Jesus didn't mind. We sat down together and talked and talked and as we did I realised what a horrible person I had become. I knew that I couldn't carry on in the same way after that. So I made a promise there and then to change my ways, to give back the money I had stolen and to give more of my money to the poor.

Interviewer: And did you keep your promise?

Zacchaeus: Oh yes! I'm a changed man now! I couldn't stay the same, not after meeting Jesus!

The two actors leave the stage.

Prayer

Dear Jesus, thank you that you gave Zacchaeus a brand new chance to start again. When we do something wrong, you do the same for us too, helping us to start again and to treat people in a better way. Amen

Songs

Songs today could include:

- 'Zacchaeus was a very little man' (Traditional)

Take home

After meeting Jesus, Zacchaeus gave much of his money away to the poor. Suggest to the children that they could think about giving something away to someone else (with parents' permission!) such as a toy or some clothes.

33 Palm Sunday

For the team

Refer to pages 6–8 to see how the activity areas work together

Session theme

As we draw close to the Easter narrative, we remember the king who arrived in the city of Jerusalem, riding a lowly donkey. This session challenges our expectations about Jesus as the promised king, and celebrates all that he is to us.

Bible text: Matthew 21:1–11; Luke 19:28–44

Team prayer

Hosanna, King Jesus! Welcome as king of our lives. Amen

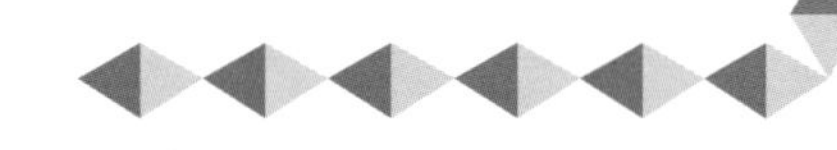

Activity areas

Small world play

Set up an appropriate scene, where children can retell the story. You could use a length of green or grey felt as a base for the street scene, together with a building-block city at one end, play figures including a donkey, and leaves and coats cut from scraps of fabric or coloured paper.

Talk about what happened that day. How do you think the people would have felt? What were they expecting would happen next?

Role play / dressing up

Provide a selection of royal dressing-up clothes such as crowns, tiaras, cloaks and princess dresses for the children to dress up in.

Talk about the way that Jesus arrived in the city of Jerusalem, not dressed as a king in a grand horse-drawn chariot, but instead riding a lowly donkey. The crowds still recognised him as the promised king.

Creative

Gather a selection of leaves in many different shapes and sizes. Provide paper and wax crayons and invite the children to create leaf rubbings, exploring the textures and shapes of the different leaves as they do so.

Talk about the people in the story who tore large palm leaves down to wave as they welcomed Jesus into the city. They were like a banner for them to wave to welcome a king.

Construction

Source an old chair and provide a selection of appropriate paints and other materials which the children can use to construct a throne fit for a king. Make sure they are wearing old clothes and/or aprons.

Talk about the way that Jesus was the long-expected king, but he came in a way that was unexpected and surprising. Jesus is no ordinary king. He came to earth to bring about God's kingdom, teaching us how God intended the world to be, unlike any earthly king or queen.

Writing

Gather a large supply of smooth pebbles and provide marker pens. Invite the children to write their own praise words on each of the pebbles—words or phrases that they want to say to Jesus.

Talk about what Jesus said about even the rocks crying out to praise him (Luke 19:40) and what this means. On that day, everyone was so pleased to welcome Jesus into the town and wanted to praise him.

Books

Set up a selection of books which retell this story and the following events of Holy Week, along with children's Bibles.

Support the children in reading the books, where necessary, and discuss with them the things that interest them.

Prayer and reflective activity

Supply a large piece of fabric, and a selection of fabric scraps and glue, as well as fabric paints and pens. Work together with the children to create a banner which could have been used by the crowds to welcome Jesus into the city.

Talk about the children's ideas as to what to add to the banner. Remind the children that when Jesus entered the city, the crowds waved palm leaves in the air to celebrate his arrival.

Story time

This storytelling makes use of the scene created for the small world play activity. Invite the children to sit in a circle around the scene so they can all see. For smaller groups, you could include them in the storytelling, manipulating and moving the props as described below, as you tell the story.

It was very close to the time of year when Jesus and his followers celebrated the Passover festival, remembering the time when God let Moses and the Israelites go free from slavery in Egypt. They arrived near the city of Jerusalem and Jesus sent his disciples to get a donkey, which they brought back to Jesus.

The disciples spread their clothes on the back of the donkey and Jesus got up on to his back, ready to ride into the city.

Position one of the play figures on the donkey at one end of the street scene, and begin moving it slowly down the street, towards the city, as you continue.

As they travelled along the road, crowds of people came to see Jesus. They spread their coats out on the ground for the donkey to walk over, recognising that Jesus was a very special person.

Place some of the felt or paper coat shapes on the road.

Then the crowds tore down palm leaves from the trees above and waved them in the air shouting, 'Hosanna, Hosanna' and 'Here comes the King!'

Use small amounts of modelling clay or tape to attach the leaf shapes to the hands of the play figures. Encourage the children to participate in the cheering.

Some local leaders tried to persuade Jesus to quieten down the crowds, as they didn't like what they were saying, but Jesus said, 'Even if these people were quiet, the stones on the ground would shout out their praise for God.'

And Jesus and his disciples entered the city of Jerusalem, at the start of a very important week.

Prayer

Hosanna, Lord Jesus! Thank you that you are the king who came into Jerusalem! Thank you that we can celebrate that you are our king, just as the people celebrated that first Palm Sunday. Amen

Songs

Songs today could include:

- 'Hosanna, Hosanna' (Carl Tuttle)

Take home

Give each child a palm cross to take home with them as a reminder of the session and suggest that they put it up somewhere in their home to remember the palm leaves that were waved when the crowds arrived in Jerusalem, and the cross that Jesus would encounter at the end of the week.

34

A very sad day and a very happy day

For the team

Refer to pages 6–8 to see how the activity areas work together

Session theme

This is the most central story of God's big story, and one that can be very difficult to communicate to younger children. During this session, we see how God transformed the situation from death and sadness to resurrection and celebration, remembering the great hope that this gives to us all.

Bible text: Matthew 26—28

Team prayer

Dear Jesus, thank you for your great sacrifice and your willingness to go to the cross for us. Help us to communicate this selfless gift to the children we work with, and the hope that it gives to us all. Amen

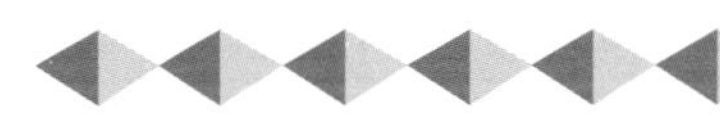

Activity areas

Small world play

Work together with the children to create a small Easter garden in a tuff spot or sensory tray, providing the materials that the children will need. These could include moss for the grass, stones to build a tomb, small wooden crosses and flowers. You could also provide appropriate people figurines for children to use to retell the story.

Talk about the story, as the children remember it, and the different feelings that people around Jesus would have had as the story unfolded.

Creative

Provide some card templates of angels (see page 126), together with a selection of different papers, foils and collaging materials, glue, scissors and paint. Invite the children to decorate their own angel shapes, using the materials provided.

Talk about the part that angels played in today's story, and what the children have discovered about angels from the Bible stories we have explored together.

Construction

Gather a selection of junk modelling materials and invite the children to work together to create a large Easter garden scene, including the empty tomb.

Talk about the children's ideas for what to include within the garden scene and why these elements are important to the story. Discuss how the women came to the garden feeling sad, but when they left they were happy and excited because they had seen Jesus.

Writing

Provide a selection of Easter cards or craft materials for children to create their own cards, along with pens and envelopes, so that children can send one to their friends or family members, to tell them a little of the Easter story.

Talk about the messages that the children could include in their cards. What can we say to share something about the Easter story with the people we are sending our cards to?

Books

Provide a selection of children's Bibles and story books which retell the events of Holy Week and the Easter story.

Support the children in reading the books, where necessary, and discuss with them the things that interest them.

Prayer and reflective activity

Lay out a large piece of paper and provide a selection of magazines and newspapers, along with scissors and glue. Ask the children to cut out different pictures of people which depict a range of different emotions.

Talk about the emotions shown in each of these different images. Ask the children how they feel about the story and why they feel this way.

Games

Gather a number of small, plastic Easter eggs, and place a selection of small items which relate to the narrative of the Easter story in them, before hiding them around the room. These could include a small toy cockerel, a piece of bread, a picture of a sword, and a cross. Invite the children to hunt for the eggs and, when they have all been found, open them to discover the items hidden inside which you can then talk about.

Story time

For this retelling, you could use four of the small plastic eggs used in the game activity. It may be helpful to number the eggs so that you retell the story in sequence. Invite the children to sit with you, perhaps passing the eggs around so that different children can share the different elements of the story.

Last week, we heard about the way that Jesus entered the city of Jerusalem as a king. Later in the week, the crowds changed the way they responded to Jesus and our story takes a very sad turn.

On the Thursday night, Jesus and his disciples were sharing a special meal together.

Take a piece of bread out of the first egg.

Later that night, when Jesus went outside to pray, he was arrested by the guards.

Take a small toy or picture of a sword out of the second egg.

Jesus was taken away, and he was questioned by the rulers at night, in secret. The crowds who had cheered for Jesus when he entered the city had now abandoned him.

On the Friday, Jesus was hung on a cross to die.

Take a cross out of the third egg.

After that he was buried in a tomb.

Take an empty egg and seal it closed.

On the Sunday, the women who were special friends of Jesus went to visit the tomb. When they got there, the tomb had been opened.

Open the sealed egg.

The women were shocked. Jesus wasn't there! When they were coming away from the tomb a man stopped them in their tracks. At first, the women thought that he was just the gardener, but he wasn't; it was Jesus!

In three short days, this story turned from being the saddest day to the happiest day. Thanks to Jesus dying on the cross and coming back to life, we all have something to celebrate!

Prayer

Dear Jesus, thank you that you died on the cross for all of us. Thank you too that you came back to life, beating death and giving us all the chance to start again. Amen

Songs

Songs today could include:

- 'All through history' (Becky Drake)

Take home

You could give each child a small chocolate Easter egg and invite them to share it with someone else, telling them about the real story of Easter as they do so.

35

Jesus returns to heaven

For the team

Refer to pages 6–8 to see how the activity areas work together

Session theme

This session explores the story of Jesus' ascension into heaven and the way that he sent his disciples out to continue his work. Through this session, we will think about the way that Jesus' message has reached us, and how we can carry on sharing the message with the people we meet.

Bible text: Acts 1:6–11

Team prayer

Dear Jesus, thank you that you are always with us. Thank you for those who have gone before us, spreading your message of love and hope. Help us to take every opportunity we are given to share your message with the people we meet. Amen

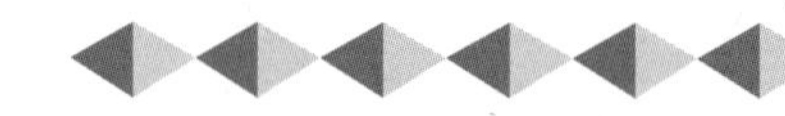

Activity areas

Small world play

Lay out a large map of the world and provide toy aeroplanes, boats and road vehicles for the children to play with, acting out taking journeys around the world from country to country.

Talk about how Jesus told his followers that they would have to speak out for him 'to all the ends of the earth'. How did Jesus' story travel from the Holy Land to us, so that we can hear his message? How can we share this message with the people that we know?

Role play / dressing up

Provide a number of backpacks, small suitcases and holdalls, along with items to pack in them, such as clothing, sunglasses, sun cream, etc. Invite the children to pack a bag for themselves as though they were about to go on a journey. You could also provide small pieces of card and pens for the children to use to create a ticket or boarding pass for their imaginary journey.

Talk about the way that Jesus was about to leave his followers to return to heaven, a journey where he needed to take nothing with him. His disciples would soon take their own journeys too, all around the world, to spread the message of Jesus.

Creative

Provide a small plain craft matchbox for each child, along with felt pens or pencil crayons, cotton wool and glue. Invite the children to create their own moving toy which can be used to retell the story. On the inside tray of the matchbox, draw a picture of Jesus. Colour the outside of the matchbox blue, before sticking a few fluffy clouds on, made from cotton wool.

Talk about the way that Jesus disappeared into the clouds. How do you think the disciples must have felt when that happened?

Construction

Set out some building blocks and base trays and invite the children to construct a model which shows something of what they think heaven may be like, or something which they think they will find in heaven.

Talk about their own ideas about heaven and sensitively address any issues this activity may raise.

Books

Display a selection of children's Bibles and books which retell this story. Other books offered today could include books around the theme of heaven, as appropriate, and atlases or maps.

Support the children in reading the books, where necessary, and discuss with them the things that interest them.

Prayer and reflective activity

Set out a simple map of the local area and invite the children to mark some of the places of interest to them.

Talk about the way that, as he was preparing to leave earth, Jesus sent his disciples to tell people about him, all around the world. Ask the children how we can do the same. Where can we go to tell people about Jesus? What things do you think are important to share about Jesus?

Games

You could play a memory game today, to remind the children that Jesus asked his followers to remember the things that they had been told, to pass on to other people.

For example, play Kim's game, where players are challenged to look at a tray and to memorise what is on it, before something is removed from the tray and they have to identify what has been taken.

Story time

This story is told through the use of fabric shapes, as detailed below, which can be displayed in front of the children, perhaps on a board or banner. Invite the children to sit down with you and set up the background board.

After Jesus had come back to life, he spent time with his followers again, reminding them of the things that he had taught them while he had been with them, and preparing them to continue his work.

Then came the day when it was time for Jesus to return to heaven. He took his disciples up to the top of a hill.

Add a felt hill shape to the board, a white figure to represent Jesus and other coloured figures to represent the disciples.

Jesus spoke to his disciples. He told them it was their turn now to continue his work without him. They would need to go out across the whole world to share God's story. Then the clouds above their heads separated.

Move cloud shapes to either side of Jesus.

And Jesus was taken up into heaven.

Move the figure representing Jesus up to the top of the board, and draw the clouds back across, separating Jesus from the people standing on the hill below.

This was the last time the disciples would see Jesus. They would never forget the things that they had learned from him, and soon they would be taking God's message out across the world. But first they had to wait for God to give them a very special gift.

Prayer

Dear Jesus, thank you for the time that you spent on earth and for the many things that you taught your people. Help us to be your witnesses in all the places you send us. Amen

Songs

Songs today could include:

- 'Father, we adore you' (Terry Coelho)

Take home

Challenge the children, when they leave the group, to think about the different places that they go to. Where can they share God's message with other people? Where can they be his witnesses?

36 God sends his helper

For the team

Refer to pages 6–8 to see how the activity areas work together

Session theme

In this final session, we celebrate the birth of the Church with the coming of the Holy Spirit upon the first disciples at Pentecost. Through this session, we find out more about what happened that day, and the way that God gives us gifts to enable us to do his work in the world today.

Bible text: Acts 2

Team prayer

Come, Holy Spirit, and fill your church with confidence to spread your story, your love and your hope with all people. Amen

Activity areas

Small world play

Provide a selection of small play figures, and playdough in red, yellow and orange. Invite the children to retell what happened to the disciples by forming small flames from the playdough and attaching them to the heads of the figures.

Talk about how the tongues of fire landed on the heads of each of the disciples and how these were no ordinary flames. Nobody was hurt or burned when it happened.

Role play / dressing up

Gather a selection of outfits from other cultures, including Indian saris and African dress. Try to include clothes which represent the different cultures involved in your group.

Talk about the different cultures and languages represented. At the time of today's story, people from many different countries were all visiting the city to celebrate a festival. God gave the disciples the ability to speak many different languages so that everyone could understand his story.

Creative

Provide a number of thin metal bangles, along with a selection of ribbons in appropriate fiery colours and different textures and widths. Invite the children to make their own fiery bangle, helping them to tie the ribbons on, as needed.

Talk about the way that the Holy Spirit touched the disciples as flames. Can you imagine what it would have been like to be there?

Writing

Provide small pieces of paper in assorted colours and felt pens. Invite the children to write down any words or phrases that they know in any other languages, to create a small display.

Talk about the different languages that are spoken by the children in your group and the different countries that they come from. How did the children learn those languages? On the day when the Holy Spirit came, Jesus' followers were given the ability to speak many different languages fluently so that they could tell other people about him.

Books

Provide a selection of books which retell the story of Pentecost, along with children's Bibles. Other books offered could include books about the Holy Spirit and the gifts and fruit of the Spirit, as well as books about different languages.

Support the children in reading the books, where necessary, and discuss with them the things that interest them.

Prayer and reflective activity

Prepare a gift box by writing the different gifts of the Spirit (from 1 Corinthians 12:7–10) on to small pieces of paper, putting them into a large cardboard box before wrapping it in shiny wrapping paper. Together with the children, unwrap the parcel and invite them to pull out the different gifts.

Talk about the different spiritual gifts and explain why they are given to people and how they are used. Talk to the children about what it means to ask God for these gifts and pray for the children, as appropriate.

Games

There are a number of games for children involving wind power, reminding the children how the Holy Spirit sounded like a rushing wind, such as newspaper fish races, where children flap a newspaper to move a paper fish along the floor, or balloon-powered cars or rockets for the children to play with.

Story time

Begin this story by asking the children if they know any other languages, and explore a few familiar phrases together. Involve all of the children in the storytelling today, taking on the roles of the disciples, beginning by standing closely together, as though in the upper room. Prepare the children to share some of their words and phrases at the appropriate point in the story.

The disciples were all gathered together in one room, just as we are now. Jesus had gone back to heaven and although he had asked his disciples to share his story with the whole world, they were feeling pretty scared.

Suddenly, as they stood together in the room, a loud whooshing noise like the wind could be heard in the room. Then fiery flames settled on the heads of each of the disciples, but it wasn't a fire, and nobody was hurt. This was God's Holy Spirit coming down into each of the disciples, giving them the confidence and gifts that they needed to do God's work.

Filled with the Holy Spirit, the disciples left the room and went out into the streets, where there were many people gathered from all around the world.

Prompt the children to move around the room.

The disciples were no longer afraid. The had total confidence to share God's message with the crowds, and God gave them the ability to speak in languages they had never spoken before, so that everyone who was visiting the city could understand what they were saying.

Prompt the children to start speaking their words and phrases.

And this was how the disciples began to share God's story with people from across the world; a story that was passed from one person to another, and on to another, until it reached us here today. And now we can play our part in passing on that story too.

Prayer

Holy Spirit, we welcome you into this place and into our lives. Thank you that you give us the gifts that we need, so that we can do God's work with confidence. Amen

Songs

Songs today could include:

- 'Father, we adore you' (Terry Coelho)

Take home

Provide copies of the gifts of the Spirit for children to take away with them as a reminder of this session and the different gifts that God offers to us, as we work for him.

Templates

All templates can be downloaded at www.barnabasinchurches.org.uk/9780857464255

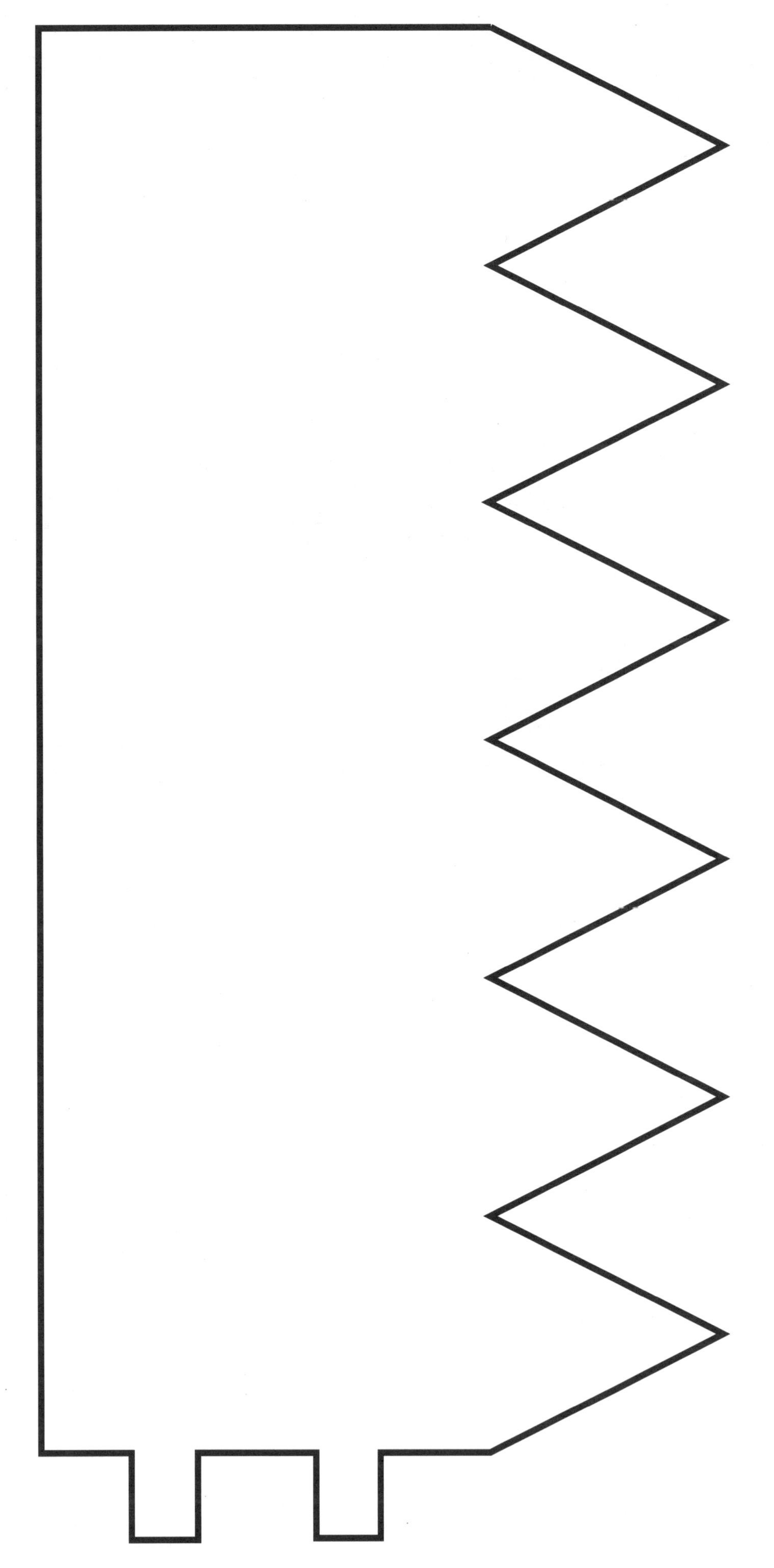

Dove

Angel

Enjoyed this book?

Write a review—we'd love to hear what you think. Email: reviews@brf.org.uk

Keep up to date—receive details of our new books as they happen. Sign up for email news and select your interest groups at: www.brfonline.org.uk/findoutmore/

Follow us on Twitter @brfonline

By post—to receive new title information by post (UK only), complete the form below and post to: BRF Mailing Lists, 15 The Chambers, Vineyard, Abingdon, Oxfordshire, OX14 3FE

Your Details

Name ____________________

Address ____________________

____

Town/City __________ Post Code ______

Email ____________________

Your Interest Groups (*Please tick as appropriate)

- ❑ Advent/Lent
- ❑ Bible Reading & Study
- ❑ Children's Books
- ❑ Discipleship
- ❑ Leadership
- ❑ Messy Church
- ❑ Pastoral
- ❑ Prayer & Spirituality
- ❑ Resources for Children's Church
- ❑ Resources for Schools

Support your local bookshop

Ask about their new title information schemes.